'88

Merry Christmas, Dad

This book comes by way of
a strong recommendation by
Dave Hawkinson. According to
him, it, surpasses the work
done by Joachim Jeremias
in the parables of Jesus.

All our love,
        Tim, Cyd, Leif
            & Eliza

*Jesus' Parables and the
War of Myths*

AMOS N. WILDER

Jesus' Parables and the War of Myths

Essays on Imagination in the Scripture

Edited, with a Preface, by
James Breech

SPCK
LONDON

First published in Great Britain 1982
SPCK
Holy Trinity Church
Marylebone Road
London NW1 4DU

Printed in the United States of America

ISBN 0 281 04008 7

Contents

The Editor's Preface: The Operations of the Imagination and the
Heart: Amos Wilder's Rhetorical Interpretation by James Breech 1

Preface by the Author 15

Acknowledgments 39

I. The Parables of Jesus and the Full Mystery of the Self 41

  1. The World-Story: The Biblical Version 43

  2. Scenarios of Life and Destiny 71

  3. Telling from Depth to Depth: The Parable
     of the Sower 89

II. The Symbolics of Jesus and the War of Myths 101

  4. Jesus and the War of Myths 103

  5. The New Voice 121

  6. The Symbolic Realism of Jesus' Language 133

  7. Apocalyptic Rhetorics 153

The Operations of the Imagination and the Heart: Amos Wilder's Rhetorical Interpretation

His North American colleagues acknowledge Amos Wilder as a major interpreter of biblical language and also as a primary source of inspiration for the flourishing of American work on Jesus' parables in the past fifteen years. And yet, until now, his published interpretations of the language of Jesus have remained scattered in learned journals or in various collections of essays dealing with religion and literature. Consequently, it has been extremely difficult for anyone other than scholars to follow Amos Wilder's quest for the meaning of this discourse. My hope is that the publication of this volume will enable interested readers to discern more clearly the distinctive contours of Wilder's rhetorical mode of interpretation, and so facilitate a more adequate understanding of the symbolics and parables of Jesus.

THE INCLUSIVE MODE OF INTERPRETATION

The work of Johannes Weiss and Albert Schweitzer at the opening of this century made it extremely difficult for subsequent interpreters of biblical language to ignore the importance of apocalyptic eschatology in the milieu which gave birth to the New Testament. In his preface to this volume, Wilder recounts his first exposure to the problem of eschatology in the New Testament at the beginning of his scholarly and intellectual career. Recognizing the significance of eschatology from the outset, he endeavored to interpret biblical language in a way that would do full justice to the particularities of eschatological consciousness.

During the first half of this century, the most widely known and dis-

1

cussed program for interpreting apocalyptic eschatology was proposed by
Rudolf Bultmann. Bultmann's view, to put it simply, was that Jesus, like
Paul and the early Christians, shared completely the mythological assumptions of his contemporaries, who thought of the world as triple-deckered
and of the End as a temporal termination. Bultmann thought of the modern man as someone who could not share the primitive cosmological and
demonological beliefs of the first century, and so attempted to develop an
interpretive system that would safeguard the meaning of biblical language
for the modern scientific man by translating that meaning into the categories of existentialist thought. This program of "demythologizing," as it
widely but incorrectly came to be known ("existentialist interpretation" is
more accurate) dominated discussions of New Testament hermeneutics
well into the fifties. Bultmann's students, largely under the influence of "the
later Heidegger," suggested modifications in the program entailed by a
richer understanding of the function of language. This modified system of
interpretation, known as "the New Hermeneutic," became the focus of debate among biblical interpreters during the later fifties and sixties. In the
seventies, the whole debate suddenly subsided (as I believe, because of the
resurgence of primitive credulity in the West), and has not been resumed.
For the past decade, there has been a seeming vacuum in New Testament
hermeneutics, but the vacuum is only apparent.

During this period, Amos Wilder continued his quest for the meaning
of Jesus' language; this book is the travelogue of that quest. As the reader
will discover for himself, Wilder's mode of interpretation reflects awareness of all the methods of biblical scholarship. In addition to the traditional
biblical tools of philology, exegesis, historical criticism, and theology, he
has included in his interpretative effort insights gleaned from an enormous
variety of contemporary disciplines: literary criticism, linguistics, the
philosophy of language, phenomenology, the phenomenology of genres in
relation to views of time, the psychology of archetypes, the psychology of
authorship, the study of dreams and folklore, anthropology, and social
psychology. And these are only the disciplines explicitly referred to in the
seven chapters of *Jesus' Parables and the War of Myths*.

The motive for this inclusive approach to the development of method
has been Wilder's conviction that in interpretation one must be as responsive as possible to all aspects of knowing and consciousness, and thus to
all modalities of man's world-belonging, including his rootedness in empirical life and relationships. Hence, Wilder's motive has been to understand language in all of its dimensions—personal, historical, and social—
or, in other words, to understand the operations of the imagination and
the heart.

From this perspective, the traditional tools of philology and historiography are indispensable, but historicist interpretation that ignores the semantic and poetic aspects of language is reductionist. Likewise, purely ideational interpretative systems (from the dogmatic to the existentialist) are reductionist when they ignore the imaginative and affective dimensions of speech, as, for example, when existentialist interpretation reduces man to his "will" and "volition." Furthermore, many types of recent literary criticism, discourse analysis, and structuralism divorce language from its concrete historical-cultural and historical-religious context, treat the text as a linguistic artefact, and so again fall into reductionism. Wilder strives to push interpretation back to the original constitution of language and its function in relating man to reality. That is his test for an adequate hermeneutics, both as regards the symbolics and dynamics of speech: to understand the operations of the imagination and the heart, one must employ an inclusive mode of interpretation.

LANGUAGE AND REALITY

When one pushes interpretation back to the original constitution of language, one discovers that language is a "primal 'gesture' of our species." Biblical interpreters must learn from the phenomenology of language, according to Wilder, "how primal an activity speech is in the human being, and how deeply linked it is with all that identifies our very being and 'world.' "[1] Reality as it is experienced is conditioned by the language available, and the language available is shaped by reality as it is experienced. Language constitutes man's "world," and language affects man's understanding of his mode of being as human. Employing a philosophical concept, one can say that language is ontologically determined.

Recognizing that language is a primal gesture of the human species has disposed Wilder to explore the ways in which basic assumptions about existence and basic modes of constituting the world determine and condition language in its more observable features, especially in the way varying presuppositions as to existence, and particular rhetorics and genres, mutually condition one another. This interest in rhetorics and genres has given his published work the appearance of belonging to the discipline of rhetorical criticism. He is accurately known as a rhetorical interpreter, as long as we recognize the way in which Wilder understands "rhetoric."

In the first place, the term does not refer solely nor even primarily to persuasion. In the second place, rhetorical interpretation as practised by Wilder does not involve the analysis of styles and genres apart from the

1. Chap. 5, p. 122.

concrete human and historical contexts which generated them. Wilder founds his interpretation on a concern with all the operations and phenomena of speech and writing as primal gestures of the human species, as deeply linked with all that identifies man's world and his existence as human in that world.

Paying attention to discrete language gestures has afforded Wilder a means of access to the specific reality-sense or world-attitude which finds expression in a particular rhetorical mode or style. He recognizes that particular rhetorics and genres condition man's presuppositions as to existence, and that man's presuppositions as to existence produce varying rhetorics and genres.

Because of this important interrelationship between man's language gestures and his experience of reality, all aspects of language and communication, including the more observable features of rhetorics and genres, change gradually together along with modifications in the way reality is experienced. The attentive interpreter will discern variations and modifications from culture to culture, and even from group to group within the same culture. It would be difficult to overemphasize that Wilder practices rhetorical criticism in a thoroughly nonaestheticist mode, because he recognizes that spoken and written genres and styles are rooted in specific historical, social, religious, and political contexts. The rhetorics that emerge from an experience of cultural continuity mean something quite different from rhetorics produced from an experience of cultural crisis, even though both may have common generic features.

The interpretative issue can be illustrated with reference to the phenomenon of biblical narrative. In his preface to this volume, Wilder reiterates his conviction that from the beginning of the biblical tradition, the "word" has been wedded to "reality," indeed to a specific understanding of reality which includes the social and historical dimensions of human existence in the world (see especially chap. 1, "The World-Story: The Biblical Version"). Biblical language is not dreamlike, in the sense of being the self-absorbed voice of the deracinated, autonomous individual. Biblical language pretends to a hold on reality in all of its dimensions.

Many academic theories of narrative presuppose the contemporary experience of personal alienation from the public arena of significant action, an experience which involves the presupposition that reality is purely subjective and inward, and hence presume that all language can be divorced from its referential context. The hermeneutical deficiency of these theories arises from their predisposition to project contemporary assumptions as to existence onto the very narratives which they propose to interpret.

This kind of misreading prejudices our understanding not only of biblical narrative, but also of apocalyptic texts. Here, "misunderstanding, as we see it, arises at a rhetorical-semantic level in dealing with the texts, at a theological level in dealing with the world views and dualisms involved, and at an historical level in dealing with the life situations which reflect themselves in transcendental vehicles."[2] The reductionist critic who divorces language from its context does not even perform the two most fundamental operations of interpretation, namely, reconstructing the life-situation which reflects itself in the apocalyptic vehicle, and conceptualizing the specific world view involved. Both historical and theological analysis are indispensable components of the interpretative process. If a reductionist critic contents himself, for example, simply with identifying ancient metaphors and mythological motifs, as do some notable practitioners of archetypal criticism, then he will miss, or, worse, misunderstand the meaning of the text, for meaning emerged quite differently in ancient literature from the way it emerges in modern literature.

Rhetorical interpretation uses the results of historical and theological analysis, but then directs its attention to the way the language of a particular text dynamically evokes response, its semantic. This is the level of interdependence between rhetorical form and world-attitude. To push back to this level requires literary insight into the interaction of form and content, but, more important, this level of interpretation requires the assistance of those disciplines which deal with the phenomenology of language and with the phenomenology of genres in relation to world-attitudes. In short, Wilder's rhetorical interpretation moves beyond literary criticism and tries to push back to the deeper structures in consciousness and to the deeper, unconscious structures which generated ancient rhetorics.

The hermeneutical issue can be further illustrated with reference to the matter of ancient apocalyptic language. The ostensible similarity between ancient and modern apocalyptic tempts modern interpreters who approach the material without sufficient historical and theological grounding, and who therefore treat the ancient texts in isolation from their contexts, to assume a degree of congruency between the worlds of experience that underlie the two apocalyptic rhetorics. Wilder shows in chapter 7, "Apocalyptic Rhetorics," that the modern catastrophic imagination, catalyzed by a collapse of confidence in civilization itself, is comparable but not at all identical to the ancient eschatological imagination which evoked apocalyptic in the first century. Ancient apocalyptic itself flourished in many different varieties and modes which should be distinguished from

2. Chap. 6, p. 138.

one another—Jewish apocalyptic and early Christian apocalyptic, for example, and the symbolics of Jesus include manifold types and subtypes. Reductionist criticism obscures important differences among varieties of ancient apocalyptic and collapses the fundamental distinction between ancient and modern apocalyptic rhetorics.

If there is such a disjunction between contemporary and ancient rhetorics and their accompanying world-attitudes, then how can one hope to understand language almost two thousand years old? Given such profound cultural discontinuities as exist between the first and the twentieth centuries, is there any principle of continuity that legitimates the task of interpretation?

Wilder is convinced that the properly prepared modern interpreter can perform an act of historical imagination and "enter into the late Jewish and early Christian mythical frame of mind."[3] There is a continuity in human nature and experience which makes this possible: "The human body has its stable form, and the human psyche is no less stubborn in its basic gestalt. There is in it something which resists any such radical change of consciousness as would constitute mania or chaotic phantasmagoria."[4] Wilder recognizes the notorious dangers of positing a continuity of any kind in human nature, but observes that the very possibility of understanding the meaning of ancient rhetorics by entering into the late Jewish and early Christian mythical frame of mind depends in large measure on presupposing some degree of deeper continuity in the human psyche as it relates to its concrete historical, cultural, and social world. Without some such permanence in human nature and the nature of society, the very names of man and society would become meaningless. There is some stability in the human psyche, Wilder believes, in spite of the important differences between the various psychological structures to which ancient and modern rhetorics speak. And the stable form of our human constitution guarantees some continuity in spite of the cultural differences in the way willing, intention, and action are related to man's social experience of reality.[5]

Wilder's scholarly style faithfully mirrors his hermeneutical principle. He has avoided the exegetical style, because, I believe, he does not want to produce a corpus of critical language that would stand in the way of the reader's entrance into the mythical mentality. Wilder's essays are designed to introduce the modern reader to a deeper appreciation of the

3. Chap. 6, p. 135.
4. Chap. 4, p. 112.
5. Chap. 5, p. 6.

dynamics of biblical language in its own historical context; they invite the reader to join in the effort of understanding the operations of the imagination and the heart.

THE SYMBOLICS OF JESUS

Bultmann used the concept of *myth* to denominate the apocalyptic eschatology of the New Testament, and proposed to recover the meaning of ancient mythological language by translating its meaning into existentialist categories. The New Hermeneutic abandoned Bultmann's basic view of language, but nevertheless continued to construe eschatological language as a word of address leading man to decision. Both systems of interpretation, according to Wilder, fail to do justice to all aspects of man's world-belonging because they reduce human reality to "will" and "intention"; they construe language only as address, and miss its semantic and poetic dimensions.[6]

When dealing with eschatological rhetorics, Wilder has employed the concept of *symbolics* in an effort to avoid the reductionist implications of both Bultmannian and post-Bultmannian hermeneutics. The term *symbolics* refers to something more than the eschatological images and metaphors themselves. "It suggests at least the social-psychological dimension of the symbol and the whole domain of cultural dynamics."[7] Eschatological rhetoric does more than convey concepts or address man's will; it is mythopoetic, meaning that it makes an "implicit claim to provide valid representation of the world and dramatization of existence."[8]

The crucible of New Testament rhetorics was an historical period of widespread personal and social crises, both in Hellenism and in Judaism. In Hellenism, the traditional myths had faded in their power to communicate meaning and to provide the basis for community. In Judaism, various groups found that the inherited patterns of Jewish life and their sanctions had been eroded by profound cultural changes. In many quarters throughout the ancient world, older ways of life were experienced as increasingly nonviable. The shaking of these older foundations and stabilities carried with it disorders on all levels—personal, social, religious, and political. This widespread sense of disorientation made anomie the char-

6. See Wilder's important critique of Bultmann and the New Hermeneutic, "The Word as Address and the Word as Meaning," in *New Frontiers in Theology: Discussions among Continental and American Theologians*, vol. 2, *The New Hermeneutic*, ed. James M. Robinson and John B. Cobb, Jr. (New York: Harper & Row, 1964), pp. 198–218.

7. Chap. 4, p. 103.

8. Ibid., p. 105.

acteristic attitude in the situation; because the traditional structures which constituted man's world were eroded, there was, for many, a consequent nakedness to the dynamics of existence.

This was the situation addressed by the language of ancient apocalyptic eschatology. The imagination of ancient apocalyptic grasped the crisis as one which renewed "the archaic crisis of all existence: that of survival, the viability of life."[9] Apocalyptic visions of the making and unmaking of the world were prompted by a corporate experience of the questionability of human life itself; the apocalyptic hierophany was prompted by a sense of man's ultimate *aporia*.

This earthly situation of faded myth and anomie engendered both Jewish and Christian apocalyptic. Both types of apocalyptic spoke to the concrete cultural situation, and both were rooted in the existing sense of reality. What is distinctive about ancient apocalyptic, according to Wilder, is that "it pioneered the first universal view of history including all peoples and times. It took history with utter seriousness, confronting the seemingly total disaster of the present and assigning meaning and hope to it in terms of the wider cosmic drama."[10] The development of a universal view of history in terms of the wider cosmic drama grows out of a world-attitude which presupposes that "there are veiled powers that live our lives; there are arcane transactions beneath the surface of experience that make fate for us; there are buried hierophanies and scenarios which are still potent in our orientation to existence."[11]

Whereas ancient apocalyptic interpreted the collapse of inherited carriers of meaning and community as a crisis of all existence, and envisioned the crisis in terms of a turbulent drama of universal history, together with a cosmic conflict of arcane powers, the modern apocalyptic imagination is preoccupied with the collapse of civilization and the apparent nonviability of personal life in the civilized world. Thus, contemporary encounters with reality have been canalized, according to Wilder, into forms of private and aesthetic epiphany.[12] Modern apocalyptic understands man in terms of freedom and choice, concentrates on his experience of deracination and alienation from the public sphere of significant action, and treats his language as impotent with respect to reality in its fuller sense.

Those who do not discriminate between the fundamental dynamics of ancient and modern apocalyptic miss the claim implicit in Jesus' symbolics

9. Chap. 7, p. 157.
10. Ibid., p. 160.
11. Ibid., p. 153.
12. Ibid., p. 168.

to provide a valid representation of the buried scenarios revealed particularly in times of acute eschatological crisis. The reductionist critic views these hierophanies in private and aesthetic terms; for him, hierophany dissolves "world." Such a view fails to grasp that Jesus' vision of the crisis of existence had to do with a crisis of recreation, not with that of catastrophe.

While the many rhetorics of ancient apocalyptic manifested certain shared world-attitudes, various kinds of ancient apocalyptic grasped the meaning of the fundamental crisis in different ways, envisioned both the historical drama and the cosmic conflict dissimilarly, and so made discrete efforts to provide some new crystallization of meaning and community. The resulting situation has been characterized by Wilder as a "war of myths."[13] The most notable contributors included several types of Jewish apocalyptic, Jewish-Hellenistic syncretism, and gnosticism, not to mention the mythopoeia of early Christianity. All of these represented efforts to respond to the crisis by gathering up the shattered fragments of inherited traditions and casting them into some new form or pattern that might establish meaning and community. According to Wilder, what characterized Christian myth and symbol was its bold encounter with the symbolic and mythical legacies of both the Jewish tradition and Hellenism. Early Christianity both appropriated and rejected powerful imagery from the Jewish tradition, and simultaneously entered into a radical and dangerous encounter with the symbolic legacy of Hellenism.

Wilder believes that Jesus' symbolics shared with Jewish and early Christian eschatology an impulse to provide "a vision of history as a whole, a transfiguration of the given world and not an escape from or a denial of it."[14] Jesus' symbolics are to be understood in the context of the ancient war of myths; the meaning of his symbolics is to be grasped in connection with his vision of palingenesis, recreation, the redemption of time and not its end.

Wilder interprets Jesus' symbolics as a transcendental understanding of his concrete historical-cultural context, a vision produced by a profound mythopoetic perception of buried scenarios still potent in man's orientation to existence in all its dimensions—personal, social, historical, and cosmic. Jesus envisions the viability of human existence in the personal sphere as having to do with earthly realities in political and social life. These earthly circumstances are perceived, in turn, as participating in

13. See "The Symbolics of Jesus and the War of Myths," pt. 2, esp. chap. 4, sec. IV.

14. Chap. 6, p. 140.

world-historical drama and cosmic conflict. Thus, Jesus' eschatological symbolics are world-representational, in that they envision the renewal of personal life together with the recreation of man's world and the reconstruction of his history.

Jesus' symbolics "give order to chaos and identify us with that which creates order."[15] Jesus identifies being human with full participation in all of these renewed dimensions of experienced reality. His symbolics therefore address man not only as conative, but also as a cultural being; they pertain to man in his full empirical involvement, and that is the key to the earthly realism of his rhetoric.

"The ultimate reference of his message and vision is that of the creation itself."[16] His vision of new modes of personal life in time redeemed and in a recreated cosmos was achieved by reordering in depth the symbolic and mythical legacies of Israel, especially the legacies of the oldest covenant imagery—the covenant of creation. Jesus' symbolics thus powerfully disclosed the deeper continuities of human reality and of man's relationship to his concrete earthly circumstance; his rhetoric was wedded in a profound manner to the operations of the imagination and the heart of Western man.

THE PARABLES OF JESUS

Readers of Jesus' parables are accustomed to look for a teaching or a theme. If the parables are thought of as metaphors, they are viewed as metaphors in the sense of earthly illustrations of transcendental truths or of religious ideas, or perhaps as easy-to-understand pictures of correct moral behavior. This way of reading the parables was current well into the sixties, when several New Testament scholars began to explore different ways of interpreting the metaphorical character of Jesus' parables.

> Now we know that a true metaphor or symbol is more than a sign, it is a bearer of the reality to which it refers. The hearer not only learns about that reality, he participates in it. He is invaded by it. Here lies the power and fatefulness of art. Jesus' speech had the character not of instruction and of ideas but of compelling imagination, of spell, of mythical shock and transformation."[17]

Largely owing to Wilder's influence, a whole generation of New Testament scholars has abandoned the assumption that Jesus' parables function in order to convey instruction or ideas, because they learned that this

15. Ibid., p. 141.
16. Chap. 4, p. 117.
17. Chap. 2, p. 83.

assumption rests on a deficient understanding of metaphor as a sign pointing to something else, such as a theme or a concept.

Wilder's rhetorical interpretation enabled him to see the parables functioning as metaphors that provide a revelatory shock of insight, as images that convey directly to the imagination a vision of what is revealed: "As with a poem, the parable form has a distinctive kind of voice, and, by its architecture, reveals rather than persuades."[18] It would not be too much to assert that Wilder's insistence that the parables function as metaphors in the sense that they are revelatory initiated a revolution in the understanding of Jesus' language. The last fifteen years have seen a lively and far-ranging discussion of the various ways Jesus' parables might be understood to be revelatory in character.

At this point, an extremely important issue emerges regarding the meaning of Jesus' parables. Are they to be understood as conveying a private and aestheticist epiphany or revelation, or are they to be understood, as Wilder's inclusive, rhetorical interpretation would have it, as revelatory of man's world-belonging, including all dimensions of reality? Many interpreters approach Jesus' parables with modern assumptions regarding the epiphanic character of metaphor:

> The epiphany moment in modern experience and the modern novel, which often has to carry the whole burden of meaning, represents a highly fragmentary grasp of reality. The momentary vision in question may have a romanticist, an existentialist, or a surrealist character, but in whatever form, it evidences a forfeiture of relationships and so of holism. It testifies, indeed, to an impoverishment of vitality in the visionary, rather than the contrary. For when epiphany is powerful, it orders reality.[19]

The experience of personal alienation from the public sphere of significant action is a distinctive feature of the contemporary situation as represented in modern narrative. Given this experience, meaning is frequently located solely in the momentary epiphany, and more often than not the vision communicated is of a fragmented reality with a subjective and aestheticist character. Inner reality is envisioned as divorced from other dimensions of human life and action. To the extent that modern narrative accurately reflects contemporary attitudes, it is valid. But is a critical theory legitimate that projects such underlying assumptions back onto the parables of Jesus? The problem is that modern assumptions regarding narrative distort our understanding of the meaning of Jesus' parables. Modern narra-

---

18. Chap. 3, p. 96.
19. Chap. 1, p. 64.

tive tends to locate meaning in the dramas of the psyche, and so many interpretations of Jesus' parables presuppose that they, too, focus on subjective reality.

Recognizing the revelatory function of Jesus' parables provides an important corrective to the usual view that they function in order to communicate ideas; however, focusing on their revelatory function alone can obscure the importance of their narrative character. Wilder notices that "to tell a story is to posit a meaningful order, however fragmentary, a degree of coherence."[20] In his interpretation of the parables, he gives full weight to their character as narratives positing coherence, and contends that the parables reflect "the unconscious assumption . . . that all life has the character of a story and of a plot, . . . the assumption that action is significant, and that the varied activities, pursuits, and vocations of men's life in nature are fateful."[21] In other words, the parables function in order to reveal a meaningful order in which not only man's perceptions, but also his actions, are significant.

The reason for this particular revelatory characteristic of Jesus' parables, Wilder argues, is that they share the legacies of what he calls biblical *epos,* whose principal characteristic is *holism.* "By this we mean the scope of awareness, the multidimensional reality and realism, the inclusion of private and public, of the inner life and the social-historical, of somatic and visionary, of ethical and metaphysical."[22]

For the biblical narrators, the crucial issue also concerned human viability, but biblical epos "provided not only orientation in the mysteries of time and existence, but therewith the structures of a human order against chaos, and of meaningfulness against unreason. The biblical epos secured life against death, being against nonbeing."[23] This does not mean that Jesus simply reaffirmed the traditional biblical view of man in every sense, but only that Jesus, like the biblical narrators and unlike most modern novelists, included in his compositions an awareness of man's multidimensional reality.

According to Wilder, Jesus' parables are not to be understood as conveying a private epiphany, but as mediating reality and life, in this multidimensional sense. True, through the parables Jesus does lead men to make a judgment and to come to a decision. But "the stories are so told as to compel men to see things as they are. . . . Sluggish or dormant awareness and conscience are thus aroused. The parables make men give atten-

20. Chap. 1, p. 54.
21. Chap. 2, p. 71.
22. Chap. 1, p. 54.
23. Chap. 1, p. 55.

tion, come alive, and face things. And they do this by evoking men's
everyday experience."[24] The parables of Jesus make men give attention to
their mundane and empirical actuality, the dimension of their experience
which, perhaps paradoxically, they most usually forget but which, the
parables insist, are fraught with significance. It is in his varied activities,
pursuits, and vocations that man decides his fate.

Others might view man's everyday experience as trivial and inconse-
quential. Jesus' parables reveal man in his earthly relationships and aspirations as "a mixture of freedom and helplessness, of loneliness and entanglement, and where all this carries with it a consciousness of responsibility,
and where man is sensitive not only to external approval or disapproval
but to internal peace or shame."[25] The parabolic metaphors of Jesus do
not function, then, to point to some other sphere of significance; rather,
they reveal man's everyday experience as the dimension where the viability
of human life is in question, where man experiences most acutely the
questionability of his existence. The parables disclose the most profound
dramas at the root of human experience where man feels torn between
anguish at his betrayal, owing to the wide miscarriage of his ventures, and
the sense of being sustained, owing to life's selective vivacity or exuberance. In Wilder's view, the parables therefore never lose their power nor
their freshness, but continue, as he puts it, to "tell from depth to depth,"
for they continue to speak to elementary human striving, frustration, and,
sometimes, unexpected fulfillment.

Jesus, according to Wilder, "dealt more fundamentally than his contemporaries with the deeper strata of human existence."[26] To be sure, his
parables reflect the power to order reality in the multidimensional sense,
but not in the sense of foreclosing the questionability of human existence.
Rather, the parables powerfully reveal human reality in its deeper strata
where man is "captured by the primordial wonder that existence emerges
out of and prevails over nothingness."[27] It is in this complex sense that
Jesus' parables are to be understood as representing man as creature poised
between anguish at life's wide miscarriage, and trust at being sustained in
his ventures; for, indeed, life's selective exuberance provokes primordial
creaturely wonder.

Both Jesus' symbolics and his parables, according to Wilder, open onto
the deeper strata of human existence. "Jesus could use such dynamic

24. Chap. 2, p. 74.
25. Ibid., p. 75.
26. Chap. 4, p. 116.
27. Chap. 3, p. 99.

images as Kingdom or Satan or Gehenna. But he could also use plot
patterns (such as lost and found) or role situations (master and servant)
which similarly engage our deepest apperceptions."[28] Since Jesus' parables, as well as his symbolics, deal so fundamentally with man's deepest
apperceptions, to understand them adequately we need a rhetorical interpretation like the one developed by Wilder—a mode of interpretation
oriented to understanding the dynamic operations of the imagination and
the heart.

YORK UNIVERSITY   JAMES BREECH
TORONTO, ONTARIO
JUNE 1981

28. Ibid., p. 94.

Preface

If there is one thing more than another which has led me to welcome the initiative of James Breech in collecting and reprinting these papers of mine, it is a continuing conviction that both scholars and general readers have failed to do justice to what one can call the operations of the imagination in the Scriptures—to the poetry, the imagery, and the symbolism.

When years ago I first began to argue this case with colleagues, both at home and abroad, I traced this limitation to a kind of professional mentality, an occupational cramp. If, in interpreting the Psalms or the Book of Revelation, they treated poetry as prose, it was because their philological tradition was interested in minutiae and analysis, while their theological tradition was interested in ideas. Even in the wider public of the churches, the poetics of the Bible were rationalized and dogmatized. Since all such imagery was sacred, it had to be "factual" in a special sense, and could not be read like any other figurative language.

While these kinds of misapprehension still persist, another more recent kind of prejudice has become widespread. Granted that the plastic and mythological elements in Scripture should be recognized for what they are and appreciated in their own terms, yet there is an unconscious premise, growing out of a long rhetorical tradition in the West, that all such discourse is somehow less serious, less grounded in truth and reality, than other more discursive styles and utterances. Perhaps tacitly the reader will say that it is "only poetry," or be persuaded that it is, indeed, a moving rhetoric, but not of the same order in Holy Writ as more direct and sober addresses and injunctions.

This lingering "aesthetic" prepossession with reference to biblical rhetorics undercuts their true force and fatefulness. Those powerful figures and figurative stories and scenarios, which speak from depth to depth, can all too easily be trivialized or sentimentalized—defused, to use an analogy

of Albert Schweitzer's—or assimilated to the arts of much literary practise—in short, to rhetorical display and contrivance. Inevitably, when the
biblical oracles and transmundane representations are thus read, whole
ranges of their meaning are forfeited. The biblical tropes and plastic vehicles evoke octaves of our human reality and fatefulness not elsewhere so
sounded and explored. Thus it is just that unique illumination of our
human lot opened up in the Bible, with its issues and horizons, which is
obscured when the poetics of the Bible are misread.

There is no need to claim that the imaginative media of the canon are
different in kind from all other picturings and fabulation. What is different
is rather the depth and richness of the soil from which they arise, the
archaic rootage and moral inventory of human nature exposed in the
annals of Israel. This orientation in existence and in history was registered
in language modes of recital and symbol which have charted the way of
our pilgrimage through many epochs.

In this legacy from the beginning, the "word" has been wedded to
"reality," and this cogency of language has applied no less to figurative
discourse. Those invisible realities which preside over the human story, its
origin, vicissitudes and outcomes, were set forth with a robustness of
representation which answered to the vivacity with which all actuality was
experienced. Our reading of these ancient texts should do full justice to
the force and meaningfulness of all such language.

Now it is true that certain recent initiatives in biblical studies have
moved to correct the misunderstandings of which I have spoken. From
social science our scholars have learned to do more justice to so-called
mythological texts and their cultural function, and not to reduce their
meaning to ideas or even to existential categories. By exposing "sacred"
letters to the kinds of scrutiny familiar in "secular" literary criticism, we
have been learning much about the poetics and rhetorics of these writings,
both their language and their message. As a result, it is more difficult
today to read the figurative and dramatic aspects of Scripture either as
prose or as "only poetry."

What I have in mind here is that whole development in our field which
we call the literary criticism of the Bible, in the sense now of concern
with its rhetorical and linguistic aspects, its genres, modes, and media.
I shall recur further on to these new strategies and the issues they raise in
connection with particular forms and texts. The point I would make at
present is that I see these earlier articles of mine here republished as still
very relevant to our ongoing tasks. It is still a question of doing full justice

to the operations of the imagination in the Scriptures, to these unique rhetorics shaped by the Spirit.

Much of our current literary and linguistic criticism of the writings still seems to me to fall short of this goal. It is a signal contribution, indeed, to have assimilated the canonical texts to general literature with respect to their rhetorics and symbolics. But should these writings finally be measured by such shared and general tests, or vice versa? When it comes to questions of human utterance, of naming and imaging, of communication, of language-and-reality, where should we begin?

The Bible is very much concerned with "word," that is, with speech, with language, in all its ramifications. Both testaments make much of the mystery of "naming" in the sense of knowing, or of calling that which is inchoate into definition and actuality. They also from of old make much of numbers and numbering, of counting and dividing, of those operations of language which map existence and orient us in its mysteries. Likewise they make much of tongues as communication, their dialogic dimension, and the distinction between Babel and sense. It is not surprising, then, that we also find a special preoccupation with all that has to do with the mystery of writing and its urgency, with books earthly and heavenly, with scrolls, tablets, scribes, and recorders.

If, as we are told by linguists, the aboriginal constitution of language involves not only speaker and hearer but also a "world" which speech is "about," then the "word" in Scripture, also in its symbolic aspects, establishes a model for the cogency of discourse. In the Bible, language pretends to a hold on reality, and is not dreamlike. We may well, therefore, attend to all its idioms, including the most figurative.

We hear much today in the conditions of our culture of the dislocation of language from reality. With this goes a widespread view in critical circles that literature follows its own laws and has its own reality, its own nonreferential autonomy. This divorce between "words and things" receives a philosophical sanction among language specialists. Those traditional frames in which we have thought to order experience—so it is urged—only obscure that much richer sensorium in which our species encounters the unknown. Existence impinges upon us through a manifold surplus of signs, swamping, as it were, our attempts at orientation. Fabulation appropriate to such an alien maze of "otherness" must forgo any *referential* claims. At best it can offer enigmatic disclosures, at the margin of meaning.

But even if one does not go so far, all such loss of confidence in language as commonly understood contrasts with the biblical use of speech.

Here, in all operations of naming and imaging, language charts the way between truth and fantasy (also called "vanity"). In its dialogic aspect as communication, the biblical word similarly establishes personal reality and exposes the alienations and evasions of the self.

If, therefore, it is a question as to what premises and methods we shall employ in our "literary" reading of the Bible, we may well hesitate before placing too much confidence in current procedures. Whatever our debt to experts in general criticism and comparative literature, we need not allow their canons to dictate our agenda. And we should not be overly impressed by the prestige of "modern classics" or the brilliancy of much contemporary investigation or "archeology of the word."

One reservation, indeed, may arise out of the orientation of much critical theory today to issues of language and rhetoric associated with the modern cultural crisis and its texts. No doubt this focus can provide its own special insights on the arts and their vicissitudes. These insights, moreover, are sharpened by new sophistications from various sciences not hitherto available. Nevertheless, much of this modern or postmodern activity is shadowed by a suspicion of cultism and Zeitgeist.[1]

This limitation appears especially when attempts are made to extrapolate its analysis backward upon the literature of the past. Why should Melville or Wordsworth be stretched on the Procrustean bed of some schema shaped to account for the disorders in contemporary letters? No doubt soundings in modern solipsist, or iconoclastic, or apocalyptic writings may be illuminated by formulas drawn from modern psychology or anthropology. But when such operations are imposed on the classics or on texts of Scripture, how much remains unaccounted for! A Freudian interpretation of the parable of the prodigal son tells us more about Freud than about Jesus. Similarly, a structuralist analysis of a parable or of a biblical recital, justified as an exploration, may illuminate its "grammar," but miss its "information" or message.

But our hesitations about criteria in biblical assessment extend to literary criticism generally. Even the main tradition of humanistic learning and letters has its own "regional" limitation, is "culture-bound." Its compass, its categories, its engagement with the human, have long been determined by a particular vein in global culture. Awareness of these special horizons has, indeed, led in comparative literature to attention to the non-Western. But from the point of view of the biblical student, the greatest

---

1. See my "Post-Modern Reality and the Problem of Meaning," a paper written in honor of Paul Ricoeur, in *Man and World: An International Philosophical Review* 13, nos. 3–4 (1980): 303–23.

issue here arises with respect to that gamut of our human reality disclosed in Scripture.

Our query to current views of literary criticism and its canons is as to whether these have not long been shaped and formulated in terms of too restricted an engagement with the human story. Even though Western literature has included a Dante, a Milton, a Hopkins, and the Eliot of "Four Quartets," and though its critics have related their humanistic appraisals to the moral and spiritual registers of such works, yet the prevailing norms have been set by a culture whose horizons and sources have scanted this depth.

The echoes in Western culture and letters of the biblical "world" with its reading of life and death are all too commonly overborne by shallower legacies, and the measuring rods employed by criticism accommodate themselves to the limited purview. It should be clear that what is called for by these queries is not some confessional or dogmatic position. A prior concern here is with language in its relation to an exhaustive and total human experience. Our disciplines and strategies with letters, our rhetorics and hermeneutics, should take account of the full gamut of speech. We should not, then, neglect the unique transactions with reality afforded in the biblical annals, in which we can, indeed, uncover an archeology of language unique in its manifold relation to our historical existence. If we wish to confront otherwise overlooked dimensions, repertoire, ranges, mysteries of language and communication, we should include this body of evidence with all others.

The literary criticism of the Bible, then, should not be only on the receiving end of secular practise, however prestigious. Biblical literary criticism has resources in its own classics which should give it a certain independence of approach. The special parameters of the biblical awareness may well instruct the mentality, the *epistēmē,* which circumscribes even our best humanistic categories and method.

In the chapters that follow, certain explorations point to this kind of enlargement of the critical agenda. The saga and voices, the epiphanies and media of Scripture open up a language-world which is not easily subsumed under our usual rhetorics. It is an old story that the texts and forms of the canon do not lend themselves to the usual categories of literary genre. More recently, it would not be difficult to identify areas of rhetorical and literary scrutiny where our biblical studies have been handicapped by borrowed formulas or premises.

One main concern of these chapters is with biblical myth and its social-historical dynamics. But a misleading formula widely current today holds that a society's myths cannot project new orientation in life's impasses, but only provide subterfuges of accommodation to them. This view, taken over from anthropology into literary criticism, only abets that existing aesthetic bias which can, for example, underrate the mythical structures in Milton or David Jones, or see them as marginal to the works.

Another focus in what follows is upon the parables of Jesus. Here a different current convention needs to be challenged. Since the parable partakes of the nature of metaphor, its interpretation will be guided by literary-critical procedure with the latter. But here again, building on an older "aethetic prepossesion," current treatment of trope and figure revels in their ambiguity and the prodigality of their implication. This free play of meaning, whether of trope, or image, or story, has a deeper occasion today in views as to the autonomy of language in general. But emphasis on the "plurivalence" of the metaphor undercuts its proper force, just as its application to the parables dissipates their particular reference. Thus the imagination is not credited with the power to name the real. It is enough that a trope or an image by its incongruity should evoke some occult depth of sensibility or hidden drama of the self.

This takes us to the chief query which must be directed to much current critical theory and practise. It has to do with the basic relation of language to reality. As I have said, a long rhetorical tradition in the West has led us to think of figurative or visionary discourse as having only a secondary kind of importance. Either as vivifying a theme or embellishing a style, there is felt to be a gratuity about these arts of speech which absolve them of referential validity or fundamental mimetic realism. Thus such rhetorics are seen as at a remove from the true nature of things. Against this background, it is not surprising that not only figurative discourse but language itself takes on in our time an autonomous character divorced from reality. It is in keeping with this that the term *fabulation* is so widely used today for all forms of literary discourse.

Those of us concerned with biblical texts and language will wish to question all such disparagement of the "word." No doubt we can appreciate the factors which have led in our period to the mistrust of traditional speech and speech patterns, as well as the quest for authenticity in fictions liberated from all such referential bonds. But in the Scriptures, the word is married to actuality and has leverage on the real. This bondedness roots, as I have observed, in the ultimate constitution of language itself. This model should leave us dissatisfied with literary and critical pursuits which overestimate the importance of language apart from its living context.

If, then, my chief satisfaction with the present volume relates to the continuing task of dealing adequately with the poetics of Scripture, this exploration also includes a number of special aspects which have interested me and which I shall wish to comment on in this preface. Perhaps the primary area of my attention throughout has been that of biblical eschatology, and particularly the apocalyptic eschatology of Jesus and his followers. This element in our early Christian writings represents a decisive feature of their mythopoesis for both the historian and the theologian, and one which calls above all for the resources of a literary criticism. Here I shall wish to clarify and defend certain of my views in the light of more recent discussion.

A further area of importance calling for continued attention to the rhetorics of the Gospels is, of course, that of the parables of Jesus. My discussion of this topic in several of the chapters which follow has been part of an extensive recent study of this form, and I welcome this opportunity to comment further on this development. But precisely this focus of interpretive method has raised questions with regard to the whole context and horizon of the literary criticism of our texts, including structural strategies, on which I shall wish to make observations.

As a preface to these later comments, and by way of providing a context for the chapters that follow, and the issues raised in them, I can think of no better recourse than to present an informal personal chronicle. Perhaps this review of occasions and encounters in the recent history of our field of study may flesh out the emergence and vicissitudes of that literary-rhetorical approach which has concerned me.

In reverting to the time of my teachers at Oxford (1921–23)—C. H. Dodd, B. H. Streeter, R. H. Lightfoot—and of my earliest teachers at Yale (1923–24)—B. W. Bacon, Frank Porter, C. C. Torrey—I am led to the observation that both the theological curriculum and biblical studies of the period reflected some isolation from wider humane initiation and method. As in the churches, nonconformist or Anglican, the theological tradition circumscribed the horizon. Philological disciplines borrowed directly from Germany or, in this country, indirectly through Moses Stuart and his contemporaries, were only rarely enriched with the kinds of humanistic breadth we associate with Eduard Norden and Franz Overbeck.

There were interesting exceptions. Torrey's charismatic book on Deutero-Isaiah would be one. Erwin Goodenough broke new ground soon after, as did Theodore Gaster, in the study of biblical symbol. Here also the work of Austin Farrer should be mentioned. But the letters of the canon were not brought into the wide purview of humane letters. It is true that these scholars knew their classics, and in this sense were humanists. Dodd, who began as a classicist and was always some kind of Platonist, did reflect this *paideia* in his biblical interpretation. But like those of other critics of his time, his efforts to modernize biblical categories did not appeal to secular literary practise. The point at which he incorporated wider insights was determined by his personal interest in the new psychology.

There was, no doubt, a connection between these limitations of scholarly method and the orientation of the seminaries and churches at the time with respect to secular culture and aesthetics. Any place in the theological curricula for literature and the arts was confined almost exclusively to the classics of devotion and to sacred music. In the course of my later visits to seminaries abroad, in the fifties, I found only two instances of offerings in the contemporary arts. At Basel, I visited a class taught by Fritz Buri in a course on modern poetry, the topic of the day being the work of the atheist poet Gottfried Benn. At Berlin, both in the Kirchliche Hochschule and Humboldt University, Heinrich Vogel, a systematic theologian who was also a musician and composer, dealt with the relation between Christianity and aesthetics.

Although many of our scholars both at home and abroad were well-read in general literature, yet such aesthetic matters were somehow derogated, for reasons related to the priority of theological concern, but also to a deeper ontological legacy in the West which influenced theology itself. The aesthetic order, imagination, and rhetoric occupied a place at some remove from the real.

To anticipate here briefly, I can illustrate by the notable case of Rudolf Bultmann. This great scholar and human being was so widely equipped that better acquaintance would commonly disallow any supposed limitations. In my visits with him, for example, I was surprised at the evidence of his knowledge of modern letters. Despite his controlling emphasis on the evangelical kerygma, he was highly appreciative of the civilizing structures of Hellenistic paganism, as of those of the modern Enlightenment. He also conceded more functional significance to the mythos of the New Testament than is commonly recognized. To that real degree that his demythologizing of this symbol meant disparagement of it, the cause must be assigned to that ontological legacy of which I have spoken, now in a neo-Kantian version. When reality and our encounter with it are identified so particularly with the conative order—with will, intention, choice, deci-

sion—the contributing operations of the cognitive and the imaginative
receive less than their due.

In this chronicle, the topic of eschatology must take a large place. Indeed,
it serves as a kind of touchstone for wider matters of interpretation. It was
in this area that I felt my first dissatisfaction with current approaches. As
I note in one of the following chapters, one could look into the main works
on this subject by Volz, Charles, Bousset, and Althaus and find no prolegomenon or section dealing with the hermeneutical or semantic problem
set by the mythopoetic character of the texts. I sought to press this issue
on colleagues in this country in my presidential address delivered to the
Society of Biblical Literature (SBL) in 1955, "Scholars, Theologians and
Ancient Rhetoric," and on those abroad in a paper at the Strasbourg
meeting of the Society for New Testament Studies (SNTS) in 1958 entitled "Eschatological Imagery and Earthly Circumstance" (included in
this volume, retitled "The Symbolic Realism of Jesus' Language," as
chap. 6). Of course the issue of demythologizing was part of the problem
on these occasions, but not the main concern.

My interest in eschatological and apocalyptic texts and mentality arose
partly from reading Albert Schweitzer's writings and meeting him at Oxford
in 1922.[2] He gave the Dale Lectures on Ethics and Civilization at Mans-
field College where I was in my first year of theological study. Because of
my knowledge of French, I was deputed by the principal of the college,
Dr. Selbie, to help Schweitzer, during his residence, with his correspondence. In Italy, at this time, I also became acquainted with Walter Lowrie,
who had pioneered in making Schweitzer's works more widely known in
England by translating and publishing, in 1913, a part of the latter's
Strasbourg thesis, *Das Abendmahl* (1901), that part whose title Lowrie
rephrased as "The Mystery of the Kingdom of God."

These contacts furthered my fascination with the myth-and-dream character of the eschatological outlook and its texts in Christian origins, and
their social-psychological import. The Schweitzer impact, however, only
crystallized an earlier preoccupation with all that is suggested by such
terms as *millenium* and *utopia*. My experience, as a soldier in World War
I, of ordeal and expectation, of preternatural transactions, of occult agen-

---

2. My chronicle at this point and a few others below parallels a fuller one entitled
"New Testament Studies, 1920–1950: Reminiscences of a Changing Discipline," writ-
ten for a collection of papers to be published in the *Journal of Religion* in honor of
Norman Perrin.

cies and *phantasmata,* all framed in glowing hopes later both frustrated and fulfilled—this experience prepared me to empathize with all such surreal symbol and its vicissitudes. I later recognized such visionary reading of history, together with the feature of an imminent climax, in analogous situations, particularly in the struggles and hopes of the English Puritans.

It therefore came home to me that an understanding of biblical apocalyptic should be sought not only in its antecedents, but in related phenomena of other periods and societies. Indeed, this alternative may be taken as a clue to the general contribution which a new literary criticism can make to biblical study. Whether we have to do with narrative or imagery, whether with a Gospel or an epistle, with a parable or an aphorism, the various forms are to be assessed not only in terms of their prehistory or immediate context, but of a total approach to language and literature. The distinctiveness of the biblical idiom and media could thus also be all the more effectively demonstrated.

The impact of Schweitzer's views here and in England was very mixed. His *Quest of the Historical Jesus,* in its German original published in 1906, had at first been enthusiastically appraised in England by W. Sanday. When the English translation appeared in 1910, Sanday retreated from his earlier view, while F. C. Burkitt, in his preface to the book, commended it highly. Most scholars sought to combine the disturbing focus of Johannes Weis and Schweitzer with more traditional approaches, but this was to forfeit the decisive contribution of the latter, identified with what he called "thoroughgoing" (*konsequente*) eschatology.

Such a view of eschatology meant, on the one hand, that, as in the case of Jesus' apparent consent to the demonological conceptions of his milieu, so we should overcome our modern standpoint and accept without qualifications Jesus' vision of the time-process. In this light, various features of his message and career would fall into place, along with seemingly disparate traits in the Gospel narratives. On the other hand, it meant that the larger picture of the beginnings of Christianity, from John the Baptist on to the early church, could be understood in terms of this key datum. Thus Schweitzer later dealt with Paul in this context.

It seemed to me that he was right in assigning such pivotal importance to this alien mythological outlook and motif and in recognizing its dynamic relation to the drama of Jesus' career and its outcomes. When I returned to Yale for the last year of my theological study, my senior thesis was entitled "Eschatology: The Rationale of Redemption" (1920). But

Schweitzer's ideas met with resistance at that time. My thesis came back to me approved, but with no comment at any point, only the signature of the reader, "B. W. Bacon."

Four years later, I returned to Yale in the doctoral program. The committee for my projected dissertation on eschatology and ethics in the teaching of Jesus included Carl Kraeling, J. Y. Campbell, and Erwin Goodenough. When I had completed the residence requirements at Yale, it was agreed that I could well get the benefit of study at Harvard, and especially suggestions from Kirsopp Lake in the further defining of my topic. In both places and elsewhere, anyone working in the line of Schweitzer was under some handicaps. I have under my eyes as I write a letter from Walter Lowrie written in 1929: "For myself I have serious counsel to give you. If you would have long life and would see good days, keep mum on the subject of eschatology . . . a subject which is highly dangerous in these days. Your teachers give you good advice: eschatology is a subject which the good and the great conspire to shun."

Although I did not myself agree with all aspects of Schweitzer's work, especially as regards the ethic of Jesus, and though one could recognize that his picture of Jesus' career was here and there based on questionable critical judgments, yet his grasp of the potent visionary media in their relation to Jesus' mission was persuasive. Schweitzer's sense of the power, not of dreams and fictions, but of deeply rooted community symbols and scenarios, threw new light on the whole drama of the Gospel story. The mythopoetic dimension of his penetration of the records can be illustrated by an aphorism in his autobiography: "The late-Jewish Messianic world-view is the crater from which burst forth the flame of the eternal religion of love."[3]

In the forties and fifties, the issues which interested me and which are reflected in these chapters moved towards hermeneutics, especially because of my contacts abroad with the Bultmannians. This was the period of the debate between Barth and Bultmann, of that between the Bultmann circle and Oscar Cullmann, the period in which Bonhoeffer's testimony was first encountered, and in which American scholars were drawn into the dominantly neoorthodox consultations of the Study Department of the World Council of Churches. Of particular interest, toward the end of this

---

3. *Out of My Life and Thought: An Autobiography* (New York: Holt, Rinehart & Winston, 1933), p. 69.

period, were the divergencies among Bultmann's followers and the emergence of the new quest of the historical Jesus. Two of my encounters with the German scholars at this time are germane to this review.

During a sabbatical year, 1958–59, I was invited to lecture at a number of German seminaries. It was perhaps a little unwonted that at Marburg a New Testament scholar should also have been invited to lecture to the English seminar. My hosts were also somewhat nonplussed that I should be in residence at the time in Oscar Cullmann's Basel, and even more so that I came to Marburg directly after a lecture at Ethelbert Stauffer's Erlangen. In the eyes of the Marburgers, I had committed the unforgivable sin of reviewing favorably Stauffer's book on New Testament theology. I had liked the way in which he ordered his presentation of the subject in terms of "salvation-history" (*Heilsgeschichte*).

My lecture to the theological faculty and students at Marburg dealt with the cosmological and eschatological imagery in Paul's letters, especially as identified with "the principalities and powers" and the "rulers" of this world. I tried to argue that Paul was here speaking in a mythological way of spiritual agencies which were also cultural and social. I urged that his categories were not simply otherworldly. If Christ had overcome these "authorities" on the Cross, and if the church was still engaged in "wrestling" with them, they were not only to be understood as such ultimate realities as Sin, Law, and Death, as Bultmann had held in his *Theology of the New Testament*. While the church was, indeed, not wrestling with flesh and blood, neither was it only engaged with theological abstractions, but rather with the actual tyrants of ancient society, whether ideological or structural. In Paul's milieu, such a world-drama could only be represented mythologically. But it seemed to me that a proper literary appreciation of the imagery should assign it some cultural and historical reference and reality. To read it only in theological and existential terms was to forfeit its dense import.[4]

In the question period after the lecture, Bultmann, who was sitting in the front row with his colleagues W. G. Kümmel and Eltester, challenged me to cite a single passage of this type in the epistles which could be taken as referring to actual historical or mundane agencies. Though the question

4. The full statement of this theme appeared in my chapter in the volume dedicated to C. H. Dodd and edited by W. D. Davies and D. Daube, *The Background of the New Testament and Its Eschatology* (Cambridge: Cambridge University Press, 1954). The chapter is entitled "Kerygma, Eschatology and Social Ethics." It received wider circulation as published separately in the Fortress Press "Social Ethics Series" (Facet Books), Philadelphia, 1966.

showed a misunderstanding of my thesis, after a moment of hesitation I quoted Paul's words:

> None of the rulers of this age undersood this [i.e., the hidden wisdom of God]; for if they had, they would not have crucified the lord of glory (1 Cor. 2:8).

The passage at least shows how transparent such terms as *archontes* (rulers) and *kuriotetes* (dominions) can be upon mundane realities. At this point Kümmel broke in, if not on my side at least to demur from Bultmann, and their ensuing discussion, to my relief, took up the remaining time.

This chronicle must include an equally revealing episode of this period, my first encounter with Ernst Fuchs. I was invited to lecture on the current situation in hermeneutics at the Kirchliche Hochschule in Berlin. Fuchs at this time was moving beyond the position in his earlier book on this topic, *Hermeneutik* (1954), and opening up his major insights with respect to "speech-event" in Jesus' sayings and in the parables, and the bearing of all this upon the historical Jesus. Though this meant a departure from Bultmann, yet the whole approach was still existentialist in a way that precluded my own special interests. For Fuchs, Jesus was more than the "bearer" of God's word (Bultmann). His sayings were "deeds" in the legal sense of a binding promise. His aphorisms and parables were linked with risk initiatives as *guarantees* of God's vindication. "Jesus was no *Dichter* [poet] but brought God to speech."

Fuchs was notorious in those days for the density and difficulty of his style, a trait well known to his students. At the same time, he was sensitive on this point. I made the mistake in opening my lecture by remarking that I could have given it the title, "Ernst Fuchs: Ein Versuch ihn zu verstehen," (thus evoking a then well-known critique of Bultmann by Karl Barth). The student audience was amused, but Fuchs was not. I meant no disrespect; I esteemed him very highly, and he and his wife had been the kindest of hosts to us. But as I found again later at the Drew Consultation on hermeneutics (1962), this talented Würtemberger was highly volatile.

To balance the portrait, I can draw on a review of a later book by Fuchs, *Jesus: Wort und Tat* (1971).

> Fuchs here puts us through the wringer again. We American pragmatists are battered and asphyxiated with his language, its idiosyncrasies and intricacies. The reader says with Paul: "Three times I have been beaten with

rods; once I was stoned. Three times I have been shipwrecked; a night and a day I have been adrift at sea." Yet the old *Meister* comes through again with compelling force. Sometimes with the felicities of a poet; sometimes with a masterly bit of exegesis; sometimes in a clarifying rehearsal of the his‚ory of critical method; but also often with a liberation of the quintessence of the Gospel.[5]

My lecture at Berlin, with its questioning of the current existentialist hermeneutics and its plea for greater recognition of the sociocultural determination of the texts and their language, could only appear to Fuchs as another example of liberal historicism. As he wrote later in commenting on the Drew meeting, referring to views there expressed by John Cobb, John Dillenberger, and myself, this approach to interpretation in terms of the sociology of religion had already long been self-evident and taken for granted in Germany. But it had only "furthered neglect of the text as proclamation," and had had to be transcended. It became clear to me in the discussions following my lecture that Fuchs's existentialist premise could not concede the fatefulness of either the contexts or the media of revelation. Behind this isolation of the kerygma from its channels lay not only the neo-Kantian ontology, but a displaced and rigid view of Law and Gospel.

This last remark should be further clarified. Whether in the case of Karl Barth and the dialectical theology, or Bultmann and his focus on the kerygma in terms of the "early Heidegger," or Fuchs and Ebeling with their similar focus in terms of the "later Heidegger," these interpreters were all rightly defending the prior Reformation witness against secularizing idolatries. On this ground, however, in keeping with their traditions, the operations of grace in common experience and of the Word in the actual language-world of men—the full import of "incarnation"—could not be carried through.

Our own "sociological" approach, on the other hand, could understandably appear superficial. Our concern with historical, social, and linguistic factors meant exposing God's word to every kind of relativity. It also seemed to them to betray an attempt to legitimate the Word and to put faith at our own disposal. But these issues could finally only be dealt with in the changing front of New Testament criticism and interpretation themselves, as the period of the "New Hermeneutic" gave way to new approaches, including especially that of the literary study of the texts.

5. "Die Näherwartung in der Verkündigung Jesu," in *Zeit und Geschichte*, ed. E. Dinkler (Tübingen: J. C. B. Mohr [Paul Siebeck], 1964), p. 45.

I break off my personal chronicle at this point. It may have been useful in vivifying the circumstances in which many of the emphases in the following chapters were formulated. I could have continued by recalling occasions when hermeneutical issues were fiercely discussed at Montreal with that master, Ernst Käsemann; or issues as to the church and the Jewish People with Abraham Heschel; or the annual meetings of the New Testament Colloquium with Hans Jonas in his home; or the more recent emergence in the Society of Biblical Literature of the Parables Seminar and its sequel in the founding of the journal *Semeia*. Throughout this period, though major activity in basic historical and philological studies was carried on, especially in relation to new-found texts, yet the chief advances in the study of Christian origins—as, for example, in the movement beyond form criticism to genre study and "trajectory" analysis— were greatly indebted to literary and rhetorical approaches.

For the purposes of this preface, I shall confine myself in these concluding pages to two areas which continue to be both important and disputed down to the present—that of the parables and New Testament eschatology. Though the texts in both cases are today dealt with in more adequate rhetorical terms, yet one can take issue at various points with much current procedure as to both premise and method.

Turning first to the parables, one can note that there are those today who for various reasons would discourage efforts to extricate the sayings from their contexts in the Gospels. By a kind of irony, some have been "overconverted" to a literary approach, and for them the part must not be separated from the whole. Thus Mark's parable of the sower must not be separated from its interpretation and other related sayings of Jesus in chapter 4. The prohibition extends, of course, to conjectural emendations of the text in any given case, attempts, that is, to restore a more "original" form of some saying. Since in the Gospels we are dealing with narrative, we should recognize that this mode has its own logic, its own overall web of connections, references, and meaning. We should not disrupt these, so we are told, by violence to the text motivated by alien and nonliterary considerations. Moreover, any supposedly more primitive version of a parable or other element in the narration can only be conjectural. We do better to confine ourselves to what stands before us as actually written and transmitted by the church.

This approach is evidently plausible. It reflects our proper new appreciation of the Gospel form, in literary terms, as having its own organic gestalt, if not as an actual genre. Thus we can also identify in a more sophisticated way that "theology of the Gospels" in terms of which the parts of any given Gospel are seen to be related to the governing perspective of its writer.

So far as the parables are concerned, this approach at least furthers understanding of them in their Gospel context, and thus in the life of the church. Those who urge it look upon attempts to identify more primitive forms of the parables as motivated by a now dated "historicist" interest. Thus in this area, as in others, there appears an unfortunate conflict between a "literary" or "linguistic" method and one that is historically motivated. It is worth noting here that those who have engaged in "structuralist" study of the Gospels, including well-known secular critics, in line with their interest in fabulation, bypass historical-referential and "diachronic" considerations. They commonly draw their "closures" in such a way as to include any parable with much else in the sections dealt with.

Those urging this literary, nonhistoricist approach to the parables find support for it in their view that in any case a parable, by its very nature, is open to many valid interpretations in differing contexts, so that nothing is really lost if we cannot reconstruct its original occasion and meaning.

Those who hold these views appear to me, as I have said, to have been overconverted to our otherwise valuable appreciation of literary and linguistic considerations in the study of our writings. In particular, they have been overly impressed by current views of the "autonomy" of language, and, what especially concerns us here, of "narrative-world." The whole question of the relation of language to reality is thus raised, and their approach moves to attenuate this. I find here an example of what I have earlier mentioned. Formulas appropriate to the situation of our contemporary crisis of meaning should not inappropriately be applied to such vital texts as those of our canon.

That parts of a Gospel, including the parables, belong together and illuminate each other and the whole is not in question. But the parts and the whole are not a self-enclosed sequence separate from the actualities which it recites or from their antecedents. The "story-world" is one face of a determining event-world. A literary reading of a Gospel should take account of its poetics, but also of its semantics, and these will evoke a lived history reaching back into the past. The evangelist and his readers, before and apart from any written Gospel, had already been shaped by a history both of language and events going back into the earliest tradition.

It is therefore not only legitimate but mandatory to search out those latent strata and motifs in Mark's narrative in terms of which the new community had been oriented and empowered from its beginning, especially where, as in the case of the parables, they lie so close to the surface of the record. This kind of investigation should not be accused of "historicism." Reconstruction of earlier forms and "language-events" underlying our Gospels is one aspect of our full encounter with what is written. The point is that "what is written," in the case of texts like these, is profoundly *referential* and does not belong only to some detached "story-world." Those who treat them otherwise, in the interest of either literary or structuralist criticism, impoverish their communication. Thus we are left with Gospels or parables deprived of their dynamics and orientation.

At various points in the chapters which follow, I urge that the biblical rhetorics, even the most figurative, have a certain robust quality, because, like the prophetic oracles in the Hebrew Scriptures or the parables of Jesus, they are rooted in dense empirical actuality. This particularity of the language should also serve as a control of our interpretation of the texts. It is in this connection that I call attention to another reservation I have with respect to current literary and generic study of the parables.

It is understandable that today, in the light of wider formalistic analysis of narrative and stories, the parables of Jesus should be correlated with analogous metaphorical anecdotes and cryptic sayings from world literature, ancient and modern, Eastern and Western. It is also welcome that universal laws and deeper patterns of storytelling should be appealed to in examination of their structure. If all such comparative studies can be furthered—and a prime difficulty here appears in the lack of agreement among structuralist workers as to procedure—we can hope that light will be shed on the parables, yet not only on what they share with other such forms, but also on their differences from them.

The reservation I would register here has to do with the so-called plurivalence of the sayings. We know that the meaning opened up by a metaphor or image can be richly indeterminate. In Jesus' parables, surprise and implication take precedence over predication. Especially when a parable is analyzed as a form apart, either because we cannot reconstruct its original occasion or because we commit ourselves to a formalistic approach, the question as to its meaning is all the more open.

But here one tendency, encouraged by "deconstruction" theory and its open view of signs and signifieds, and stressing the aspect of plurivalence, is to extract the parables from their historical context in the Scripture altogether, so as to relate them to modern literary or oriental paradoxes and riddles. Thus their import may be identified with some supposed iconoclastic or enigmatic wisdom. Deconstruction, indeed, looks for some "carnal" speech anterior to our inherited language categories or for arcane disclosures mediated by the antinomies found in all experience and discourse.

Another, less radical procedure would, indeed, safeguard something of the original meaning of a parable by insisting on its "shape" and poetic as a control, while prizing its plurivalence as that which gives it relevance for readers in different situations and with ever-differing approaches. But how safely can the full meaning of these communications be identified with their shape and plot apart from the horizon and ambience in which they arose? Here again, language such as this must not be divorced from its referential context.

If we urge that the thrust of a parable, as of any rhetorical genre, should always be controlled by its acoustics in a particular "linguistic community," and if we would thus guide our interpretation of a parable in terms of the expectations of those who heard Jesus, we may be accused of a "genetic" approach looked on today as both dated and impossible. But this surrender to literary and synchronic tests, as against historical-diachronic, ignores the continuities of life and language, and the ways in which the past both determines and nourishes the future. The quest for the historical Jesus and his utterances is, indeed, difficult. But the church has always lived in relation to these, especially in its depths. Appeal to this past which is also present—an appeal in which written traditions and latent testimony and norms control each other—need not be viewed as historicist. Our scholarly operations in bringing those formative phases and events to light are not rationalistic, but an appropriate clarification of the church's life and memory.

The conflict in some quarters today between a literary-linguistic and a historical approach to our writings should be resolved by a better understanding of both. The former leaves us with free-floating texts which move toward gratuity and fantasy. The latter evacuate the recitals of their full import in the quest for facts and thematics. What is called for is a literary method which takes better account of the relation of language to reality, understanding reality, however, also in its historical dimension. In the case of our New Testament writings, this call is above all urgent. For these forms, images, and myths answer to a particular empirical reality, the Gospel, and our reading of them should take account of their embeddedness in this dynamic movement. This means that all of the language forms should be studied diachronically and in terms of trajectory, so better to interpret any particular synchronic stage in which they may have been transmitted.

These observations about current study of the parables are so brief and selective that they may appear to do an injustice to scholars who have worked on these frontiers. I would therefore wish to register my special tribute to Dan Via, Robert Funk, Will Beardslee, and Dominic Crossan, among others, who in various ways have explored this new territory, and to whom I am in so many ways indebted.

For my final comment, I return to my prior concern with eschatological imagery and its interpretation. I find it interesting that colleagues tell me from time to time that they find my views in my early book *Eschatology and Ethics in the Teaching of Jesus* (1939, 1950) more satisfying than such later studies as those by W. G. Kümmel and Norman Perrin. I believe that this agreement points especially to my attempt to understand the apocalyptic-eschatological outlook, including its focus on imminence, in terms both social-psychological and imaginative. In this light, the mythological expectation of Jesus could be seen as both historically realistic, as regards the fatefulness of his times and errand, and yet transparent upon an ongoing world, only implicit, indeed, in the total vision, but subject to its norms.

My view was understandably but mistakenly classed in the German discussion with those which sought to evade Jesus' expectation of imminent judgment and salvation. It was a question, however, of language and of coming to terms with "mythical mentality." My position was not the same as that of those who sought to expunge sayings which stressed the imminence of the end. Neither should I have been classed with those who defended a "realized," rather than a "futurist," eschatology.

The discussion of the imminence of the Kingdom from Kümmel down to Perrin and Erich Grässer has unfortunately been handicapped by a flat conceptuality which has obscured the issues. Kümmel maintained what one can call the abstractly correct view that "Jesus reckoned with the near future of God's reign within the limits of his generation . . . and in this expectation had been misled."[6] But it was just such rationalist categories which led many to demur and, with the same anachronism, to find a way out by holding that (in Kümmel's words) "Jesus' proclamation of the near reign of God stood altogether apart from any temporal connection, that Jesus rather ignored time since the vertical dimension of the Spirit cannot be temporal."[6] This view, which Kümmel opposed, he assigned to Fuchs, E. Jüngel, H. Conzelmann, and Perrin, among others, the last of

6. Ibid., p. 32.

whom observed, "We may not interpret the eschatological teaching of Jesus in terms of a linear conception of time."[7]

Both Kümmel and those he opposes are caught in an anachronistic formulation of the matter. We may be sure that in his own horizon and idiom, Jesus did reckon with time most responsibly. Those who, denying this, would thus escape the embarrassment of the interim message are like those who either Platonize it or existentialize it: these all subvert, in one way or another, the full force and meaningfulness of Jesus' plastic forecast. Even Norman Perrin, though in his later writings he espoused a literary approach (recognizing the Kingdom of God as a "tensive symbol" evoking "the myth of God acting as king"), subjectivizes the import of the eschatology, as when he writes: "The challenge of the message of Jesus was to recognize the reality of the activity of God in the historicality of the hearer's existence in the world, and especially in the experience of a 'clash of worlds' as the hearer came to grips with the reality of everyday human existence."[8]

What one misses here is the massive reality of cosmic transformation evoked by Jesus, and related not only to inwardness, but to time and place. The "everyday human existence" in question was not just a matter of "historicality," but was set in a theater of world-palingenesis. The persuasiveness of Jesus' scenario lay not only in its antecedents in Israel's national hope, but, especially for his followers, in its correspondence to the Hellenistic and Roman dream of a cosmic *eirene* or state of harmony. Very relevant to this understanding of early Christian eschatology has been Ernst Käsemann's insistence, against traditional theological views, that the "righteousness of God" mentioned in Paul's letters, in its operations, should be understood in cosmic terms.

Whether with respect to the parables or to the eschatological imagery, it is one thing to do justice to their figurative mode and imaginative resonance. It is another to raise the question as to their correspondence with reality. The arts of language, the fabulation, the stories, the poems of mankind have always had some kind of ground in things as they are or as they are experienced, however fictional the transcription. It has been a main concern of the chapters which follow to insist upon the distinctive

7. *The Kingdom of God in the Teaching of Jesus* (Philadelphia: Westminster Press, 1963), p. 185.

8. *Jesus and the Language of the Kingdom* (Philadelphia: Fortress Press, 1976), p. 196.

way in which the rhetorics of our canon, even the most transcendental, are determined by mundane and empirical actuality, all in the light of Israel's mapping of our existence—a "humanism" more searching, more disabused, and yet more hopeful than our Western humanism at its best.

Any claims today which link language with reality, words with things, and which do not distrust the acts of naming, predicating, and imaging, meet with a proper suspicion. Our semiologists and deconstructionists urge, as I have noted, that the world-mystery impinges upon us by such a plethora and excess of signs that our attempts to chart them in terms of some center or origin can only be arbitrary. Those "frames" of reason or spirit by which we order existence are self-flattering, and our inherited pictures of the unknown are illusory. Indeed, the exposure by such language philosophers of the deceptions of language reminds us of the Hebrew prophets who spoke of the oracles of the peoples as lying visions, the false imaginations of their hearts, as vapor and ashes.

To argue the cogency and reality-sense of early Christian eschatology, we can find a kind of acid test, therefore, in the categories of such a deconstructionist as Jacques Derrida, and I propose briefly to examine the Book of Revelation in this light. What makes the Apocalypse appropriate here is the fact that its discourse draws upon a vast and labyrinthine repertoire of occult "signs," imagery, scenarios. Wide-ranging and recondite transactions of human consciousness with existence, including those of many societies, are invoked: cosmological, astrological, meterological, theriological, chthonic, numerological, as well as those identified with ancient historical dramas. Yet we do not have only a phantasmagoria. This language does not run free out of control, or out of relation to life and history. Nor are the recitals and hymns vacuous, dreamlike, gratuitous. What we have here is a mastery of language in all its ambiguities, and a grip on the real.

This rooted cogency of the work runs through all its parts and can be identified in the detail of their style and poetic. Its mosaicked utterance throughout is nourished by an urgency which shapes the recitals and lends coherence to the whole. The voices and visions are penetrated by an intelligence which relates them to life. A recurrent error in literary criticism is that which would assimilate the literary arts to the nonreferential art of music. Those who today, like the deconstructionists, would insist on the autonomy of language carry this misunderstanding to its limits in their goal of an "erotic" language.

A further "acid test" set by such linguists as Derrida and Roland

Barthes for a writing like the Apocalypse bears on the "persona" of the author. For much modern analysis of narrative, the nonreferential autonomy, and in this sense irreality, of the language has its counterpart in the elusive identity of the "I" or subject from whose point of view a work is projected. But it would be difficult to dissolve the "I John . . . who heard and saw these things" into a theatrical or fictive persona. With many writings, we are told, one can look behind the mask of the narrator and find no real author but only one who is "a mere function of the language-system." It is not surprising that we encounter today the expression, "language writes." The authorial urgency and realism are lost sight of when the "fictional world" is thus assigned autonomy.

Certainly there is nothing theatrical or masklike about the untitled scribe of this writing, whose empirical reality is identified with the actuality of his community and its ordeal. The language, the play of symbols, the communication, all are anchored in and controlled by this personal and historical realism. After all, it was to nerve a community to persist in the terrors of martyrdom—and thus to overcome the most rooted instincts of human nature—that he marshalled his spectrum of language. The sanctions, motives, and models of such an appeal in such a juncture are, indeed, by social scientists, brought under the caption of "social control." But John's total constellation of language goes far beyond any such prudential inducements to a world orientation founded in faith and history.

As if to counter any charge of merely inventive or gratuitous fabulation, we observe that this writer is particularly concerned with the act of *naming* and its ultimate authorization—of calling agencies by their real or new names; with the sanctions of *writing*—the authority behind scroll and letter; with the force of *speech* as resembling a two-edged sword, and as having the character of decree and *fatum,* rather than that of idle eloquence; with the validity of *witness* and the distinction between truth and illusion.

This dynamic "word," grounded in actuality, shapes the entire work both in its detail and in the masterful architectonics of the whole, such that the *alta fantasia,* as in the case of Dante's *Divine Comedy,* is throughout wedded to reality, especially by the dialogic dimension of the discourse.

The author of this writing, therefore, is not fictive, and his language is not alienated and gratuitous. This scribe, rather, recalls the familiar image of the giant who holds in his fist a sheaf of arrows representing lightning bolts. Above all, there can be no question—with our deconstructionists—of "decentering" the discourse. This mythopoetic transcription of an encyclopedic world-drama has its center, not in the obliquity of some fabulist's stance or in the vagary of some cultural horizon, but at the focus of Alpha and Omega.

I have sought to illustrate by the example of the Apocalypse the ways in which early Christian eschatology was grounded in reality—not only in historical actuality, but in the nethermost piers and caissons of human being itself. It is this matrix of our canonical texts which determines the convincing and convicting force of the language, which is something more, as I have urged, than its rhetorical resonance. Jesus and his followers prevailed over the cultural options and resistances of their rivals because their "symbolics" answered more fundamentally to the quests of the time.

Of course their witness was not by word alone. But the point here is that this "word"—its distinctive idiom, syntax, voice, its communication modes and speech registers—had an operative, enactive character. As the author of the Epistle to the Hebrews wrote, "The word of God is living and active" (4:12). The language itself, apart from its topics, was life-related, somatic, engaging. Thus the witness in word was inseparable from the witness in action and behavior.

If, then, we can see the theater of Christian beginnings in terms of a "war of myths," one can identify it even better as one of liturgy against liturgy or liturgies, with the understanding that liturgy involves a whole life style, action and ethic as well as recital.[9]

In speaking of the ultimate matrix of our writings and their language, we are no doubt pointed to the problem of "structures." Like all texts, those of Scripture betray ancient vicissitudes of conceiving and imaging, ancient strata of naming and telling. In our current exploration of structures in narrative, in myth, in language itself and its archeology—apart from whatever valuable penultimate analysis is carried out—it is all too evident that the search ends for many only in indeterminacy or ultimate antinomies. In either case, apart from nihilism, a current resort is to some form of gnosticism. Thus the same alternative reappears today which the church confronted in its beginnings. As ever, the issue concerns the power of language to name and image the real.

In closing this preface, I wish to express my warm appreciation to James Breech for his initiative with respect to this volume, and for the perceptiveness and care with which he has selected and presented its contents. From

---

9. Cf. my *Theopoetic: Theology and the Religious Imagination* (Philadelphia: Fortress Press, 1976), pp. 26–30.

his days at Harvard as a student, I have always found his approach to our studies congenial and have valued his contributions highly. I also wish to thank the original publishers of these chapters for their permission to reprint them in this collection.

HARVARD DIVINITY SCHOOL   AMOS N. WILDER
CAMBRIDGE, MASS.
FEBRUARY 1981

Acknowledgments

Grateful acknowledgment is made to the following publishers for permitting us to incorporate previously published articles and essays as chapters in this book:

Chapter 2, "Scenarios of Life and Destiny," is reprinted by permission of the publishers from *Early Christian Rhetoric: The Language of the Gospel,* by Amos N. Wilder (Cambridge: Harvard University Press, 1971). Copyright © 1964, SCM Press-Harper & Row; Copyright © 1971 the President and Fellows of Harvard College.

Chapter 3, "Telling from Depth to Depth," is reprinted by permission of the publishers from *The Good Samaritan (Semeia* 2 [1974]: 134-51), edited by John Dominic Crossan (Missoula, Mont.: Scholar's Press). Copyright © 1974 the Society of Biblical Literature.

Chapter 4, "Jesus and the War of Myths," is reprinted by permission of the publishers from *Myths, Dreams, and Religion,* edited by Joseph Campbell, pp. 68-90 (New York: Dutton, 1970).

Chapter 5, "The New Voice," originally entitled "Eschatology and the Speech Modes of the Gospel," is reprinted by permission of the publishers from *Zeit und Geschichte: Dankesgabe an Rudolf Bultmann zum 80. Geburtstag,* edited by Erich Dinkler, pp. 19-30 (Tübingen: J. C. B. Mohr [Paul Siebeck], 1964). It appears here in a revised form.

Chapter 6, "The Symbolic Realism of Jesus' Language," originally entitled "Eschatological Imagery and Earthly Circumstance," is reprinted by permission of the publishers from *New Testament Studies* 5 (1959):229-45. Copyright © Cambridge University Press.

Chapter 7, "Apocalyptic Rhetorics," originally entitled "The Rhetoric of Ancient and Modern Apocalyptic," is reprinted by permission of the publishers from *Interpretation: A Journal of Bible and Theology* 25 (1971): 436-53.

Unless otherwise noted, biblical quotations are from the Revised Standard Version of the Bible, copyrights 1946, 1952, © 1971, 1973 by the Divi-

sion of Christian Education of the National Council of the Churches of
Christ in the U.S.A. ahd are used by permission.

Editor's Note: In the following essays a number of footnotes lack certain
information—full facts of publication and so forth. Complete references
were inaccessable either to author or editor at the time of the preparation
of this volume.

I

THE PARABLES OF JESUS AND THE FULL MYSTERY OF THE SELF

1

The World-Story: The Biblical Version

... si l'un de nous avait eu la tête épique!
                          Proust, *Du côté de chez Swann*

Tell all! Tell all!
                                   Beckett, *All That Fall*

I. MODERN SUBJECTIVITY

A proper theological assessment of literature should direct itself first of all to matters of language and rhetoric. But also the theological critic could well take account of the literary heritage of his faith and its special modes of language. If one considers the momentous influence of the Hebraic and early Christian writings upon Western culture, we cannot but be struck by the anomaly that in general literary criticism such small attention has been paid, relatively, to these antecedents at this level. The fact that these classics have been assigned to the category of sacred texts has meant that their specifically linguistic and rhetorical features have not received the kind of attention in the study of letters and of comparative literature that have been given, for example, to the Greek classics.

Our purpose in the present chapter is to observe certain features of Hebrew narrative and use these as tests or queries directed to contemporary narrative or fiction. It is to be granted that the writings in question are separated by millenniums in point of time and by other radical disparities. But if we approach the task as a scrutiny of language, disregarding formal dogmatic considerations, my proposal may have some justification in the modern interest in the study of genres, in comparative rhetorics, and in the ultimate shaping of our language and apperceptions by the biblical texts.

I shall be concerned with style and rhetorical modes, and with the kinds

43

of realism or particular reality-sense associated with them. But my project also offers an opportunity to reflect upon the dilemma of the epic form in our period, or at least on such features of epic as may have an afterlife in our changed world. This topic is one that well highlights the special character, if not the limitations, of modern narrative, and may well, therefore, be briefly considered at the beginning of the discussion.

The larger cycles of the Old Testament histories represent a kind of epic, as we shall see in what follows, and Milton, for one, could base his Puritan-humanist epics upon the biblical storytelling. It is generally recognized that the conditions of our own period are not propitious for any such larger plotting of experience. Yet the modern writer is attracted to the older epics, as he is to Greek tragedy or to archaic mythical patterns, and we can detect a deep impulse even in the midst of our age of incoherence to achieve some universal pattern of fabulation by direct or indirect appeal to the structures of Homer or Dante or the Bible.

There is something poignant about the struggle to relate our modern anomie to these older stories of man, for our climate is surely uncongenial to such confident world-recital as those of the *Odyssey* or the *Divine Comedy*. We have here on one scale—in the work of Joyce, or Pound, or Proust—examples of that wrestling for meaning which in the less ambitious scope of most novels seeks through a close recital of experience and events to throw light on the enigmas of some more particular life-drama.

When we think of the major epics of the past, we recognize a large-scale kind of recital in which the particular self-understanding of a society or an epoch is evoked, and one which gives order to its experience of time, in particular. All such narrative chartings of experience presuppose a confident and naive sense of communal and world reality. But it is just here that our modern fictions have a different, if not more limited, scope.

We may illustrate by the case of Gertrude Stein, who was all her life interested in the problem of narrative in our age, especially in America. She called her *Making of Americans* an "epic" and related it to Joyce's *Ulysses* and to the work of Proust. What makes this case especially appropriate here is that she also cited the Old Testament, praising it as an analogy of her idea of contemporary narrative, as against the kinds of narrative that have obtained in the past.[1]

---

1. *Narrative: Four Lectures* (Chicago, 1935), p. 19. Note the remarks of Carl Van Vechten in a letter to her about *The Making of Americans*: "To me, now, it is a little like the Book of Genesis. There is something Biblical about you, Gertrude. Certainly there is something Biblical about you." Cited by Elizabeth Sprigge, *Gertrude Stein: Her Life and Work* (New York, 1957), p. 135.

What Stein meant by "epic" and how her definition suits or departs from the classic understanding appear in the character of her book and in her general reflections on narrative.

The *Making of Americans* began as a thinly disguised history of three generations of Gertrude Stein's own family of Jewish immigrant stock, grew to include the histories of everybody the family knew, and ended up as an attempt to encompass the history of "all who ever were or are or could be living," described according to "personality traits." For the author, the "bottom nature" of human beings, the reflexes of the complete characters of individuals, were reflected not in their words and thoughts, but in the movement of words and thoughts, "endlessly the same and endlessly different." Yet she also emphasized that there is a hero in the work and a hero who dies.[2]

In her lectures entitled *Narrative,* Stein clarifies her intention as a way of writing which deals with reality as "immediately existing" and as immediately "known" in the recital, rather than told at a remove. The excitement lies in the lived apprehension of the actuality of things and events. While there is sequence in any narrative, it is not the important thing, and she especially decries the banality of the pattern of beginning, middle, and ending. What is especially surprising here is her view that

> in a kind of way what has made the Old Testament such permanently good reading is that really in a way in the Old Testament writing there really was not any such thing there was not really any succession of anything and really in the Old Testament there is no sentence existing and no paragraphing, think about this thing.[3]

In the Old Testament, she writes,

> They told what they were and they felt what they saw and they knew how they knew and everything they had to say came as it had to come to do what it had to do.[4]

Evidently, Gertrude Stein's view here appears to fly in the face of the usual view, and one which we shall stress later, that the narrative of the Bible takes time and its events seriously and, above all, provides a world-plot, with a beginning, middle, and end. But her emphasis on reality in "existing" and on language as event in the now has its parallels even in theology today. We have here, in any case, a good specimen of the direc-

2. "Announcement of *The Making of Americans: The Complete Version*" (New York, 1966). Cf. T. N. Wilder, introduction to her Four Americans (New Haven, 1947).

3. *Narrative,* p. 19.

4. Ibid., p. 27.

tion in which the man and artist of our time, conditioned by modern subjectivity, seeks a different kind of structure for epic or for any major narrative work than has been used in the past. Moreover, we recognize in Stein's way of putting it the modern revulsion, so clearly stated and practiced by D. H. Lawrence, against the staleness of the usual plot of good and bad fortune, and the determination to go deeper into psychological or moral constants.

These observations on the fate of the epic mode in our day lead me to a theme that is basic to my further discussion. For better or worse, the problems set for men in the West have long focused upon what we speak of as his subjectivity, and this has been increasingly true with the passage of time. This category has many facets, and its sense varies in different contexts. In the present connection we have been led to it by the contrast between a public arena of significant action in time and a more inward one. This is related to the loss of authority of older social and cosmic assumptions and their structures, with the result that meaning must locate itself in the dramas of the psyche. From the negative point of view, emphasis can be placed on the accompanying loss of the sense of the reality of the world, and the alienation of our *unbehauste Mensch*. From the positive point of view, the emphasis may fall on the liberated powers of the self.

The consequences for literature and its genres have been correspondingly diverse. Not only is the individual artist conditioned by his own particular form and degree of exposure to the cultural shift, but various aesthetic and philosophical versions of the situation have their influence: surrealism, apocalypticism, psychologism, existentialism. The main point to bear in mind, however, is that all such psychodrama and creativity seek contact with the real. The order of art itself presupposes a wider order. And any such rediscovered ceremony and orientation must have their profound correspondences with those of the past. In this sense, the words of Herman Melville may guide the promptings of the modern artist:

> Not innovating wilfulness,
> But reverence for the Archetype.[5]

In this connection we could recall one recent poetic narrative of epic scope which takes public history and its successions seriously and links the import of private experience with a world-plot, and that is *The Anathémata of David Jones*,[6] which is at once a cult-epic and a celebration of *homo faber*. Here the achievement is all the more remarkable because this

---

5. *The Works of Herman Melville*, vol. 16, *Poems* (London, 1924), p. 287.
6. New York: n.d. (English edition, 1952).

rehearsal of man's ceremonies and technics is the work of one thoroughly
initiated into the modern sensibility. One evidence of this is the specific
acknowledgment he makes to Eliot and Joyce in his preface. The work
may be taken as one clue to the various solutions sought today both in art
and in life in the attempt not to transcend psychologism and subjectivity,
but to exploit what we may learn from them for the sake of more adequate
structures.

Although I intend to deal with the biblical material in this chapter in a
nondogmatic way, I nevertheless invite the reader once again to look upon
the undertaking as an exploration in theological criticism. In focusing
upon the language, I am not conscious of surrendering my confessional
premises. I am going behind doctrine and confession to their matrix in the
life process and its recitals, to the biblical humanism which nourished the
faith.

Theology, in any case, often neglects this subsoil of the tradition, and
in two senses. Its changing formulations may proceed without constant
reimmersion in the elemental experience of man precisely as here narrated
and fabled. What Christianity is taken to be, in various periods, forfeits
its continuity with the fateful early vicissitudes of the people of God at the
quasi-secular level, especially as evoked in the older annals. More specifically, biblical theology operates selectively in its appeal to Scripture.
What is taken as normative for faith, and therewith for liturgy and ethics,
tends to abstract from the wholeness of the canon. Thus the substance of
Christianity is spiritualized, not only by a focus on the New Testament at
the expense of the Old, but in the Old Testament itself by a neglect of
those generically human strata represented by the narrative, as well as the
wisdom deposits.

Thus theology tends to shortcut the concrete human givens that are
basic to doctrine, especially as they are manifested in the Old Testament
storytelling. But such obscuring of the "human nature" in the Bible immediately frustrates any proper grasp of the relation of theology to culture,
and particularly of theology to the arts. The plain reader of the Bible,
nourished on the stories of the Pentateuch and the books of Samuel and
the episodes in the Gospels and the Book of Acts, is already initiated into
an implicit theology all the more negotiable in his own setting for being a
matter of vivid story and poetry, rather than of abstractions.

It is in the biblical epos, especially in the older records, that we find
ourselves face to face with man as the arts also reveal him, man the creature, man the maker, symbol-maker and fabulist, and man the political
animal. The arts also are directly concerned with natural man and his

endowments and dynamics. No theology will be adequate that obscures these. It is true that Hebrew man is distinctive. There are many differing humanisms, and we have here one remarkable instance. The unique narratives and epics of different peoples and ages expose all such differences in a most revealing way. This is clear in the case of the biblical epos, and the differences can serve as an appropriate basis for theological criticism of narrative literature generally.

To anticipate by one example: Let us suppose that one thing we look for in an account of some course of human events, fictional or not, is completeness[7]—not necessarily quantitative, but the full dimension of the event, with some suggestion of its deeper and wider context, and of those significant intangibles so easily overlooked. We cry out to the reporter, "But that's not the whole story! Tell the whole story!" As Mr. Rooney charges his wife in Beckett's *All That Fall,* "Tell all! Tell all!" May it not be that biblical storytelling will provide a test here?[8]

In the next section (II) we shall introduce the claim that the Hebrew epos, as compelling language and world-story, in its combination of realism and holism, has served countless generations as a "house of being" or cable of order and survival across the centuries. And we shall confront it with the understandably restricted scope of contemporary rhetorics. In following sections, after noting the prominence of the narrative mode in Israel's Scriptures and its relation to this people's self-understanding, we shall consider more in detail the world-plot character of the narrative cycles, or movement from first to last things (III), the richly concrete historical realism of the narratives (IV), and matters of style corresponding to these features (V). We shall be led to observe that the ultimate motivation of the biblical recitals and the urgency of the fabulation are associ-

---

7. Gertrude Stein, again, witnesses to one version of this, for it is in connection with her method in writing *The Making of Americans* and her attempt to get at the "bottom nature" of men and women that she explained, "When I was working with William James, I completely learned one thing, that science is continuously busy with the complete description of something, with ultimately the complete description of anything with ultimately the complete description of everything." Cited by Elizabeth Sprigge, *Gertrude Stein,* p. 73.

8. In the case of Mr. Rooney, to "tell all" is to not omit the fact that the baby in question fell under the wheels of the train. Beckett wants, among other things, to rebuke dishonest sentimentalism and pietism, as suggested by the ironic use in his title of the words of the psalm, "The Lord upholdeth all that fall" (Ps. 154:14). When the Christian asks that the whole story be told—"Tell all!"—he also insists with Beckett that all such fatalities be told without blinking them. But in the demand "Tell all!" he expects a great deal more. In fact, he may precisely ask the narrator to do justice to the insight that "the Lord upholdeth all that fall." As a matter of fact, Beckett himself does not shut his door finally, and is by no means the voice of despair and derision that many critics suppose.

ated with defense of the human order against chaos. It is this also which drives the narrators to some kind of total history, both in scope and in empiricism. So we are led to ask (VI) what relevant queries can be brought from this kind of storytelling to contemporary fiction. In particular, we shall observe that there is a striking analogy between the biblical rhetoric and that dimension of personal reality (intentionality, dialogic movement, cf. dialectical or epic theater) which emerges as so telling a feature in much recent work.

II. BIBLICAL HUMANISM

Modern man lives with an increasing burden of subjectivity, at the expense of his sense of the reality of the world.

Susan Sontag, Against Interpretation

A theologian reflecting on the modern novel may well find himself driven back to a review of the whole phenomenon of storytelling and recital as one of the primordial modes of language. The prominence and character of this vein of rhetoric in a given society is a significant index of the culture. Those concerned with theology and literature will ask themselves especially about narrative genres in various religious contexts. The biblical theologian will naturally be led to scrutinize the special role of narrative in Scripture, beginning with its dominant place in the literature of Israel.

Since we put modern fiction under the microscope and bring to bear upon it so many diverse interests, it is surely not farfetched to invoke the biblical narrative as a foil and see what observations may be forthcoming. Indeed, we may here find ourselves on the track of a theological criticism more appropriate than some others. In assessing any particular literary form, certainly one appropriate test should be that of any corresponding Christian or biblical genre. It is to this end that we make a first appeal, not to dogmatic tests, but to the Hebrew recitals, their styles and rhetorics. Here we can operate at a literary level rather than a theological, or, better, we can operate theologically at a literary level. Rather than test the modern novel by biblical truth, let us test it by biblical storytelling.

We have in view here, first of all, the narrative of the Old Testament, beginning with the Pentateuch. Again one will ask: If we leave out theology and confine ourselves to this narrative as a literary genre, how can we profitably compare it with the modern novel, after almost three millenniums? Yet let us remember that even in the smaller units of storytelling there are significant differences, morphologically, in the stories of different cultures. And we can look farther. When Erich Auerbach compares bibli-

cal and classical narrative units, he includes more than style in the narrow
sense. Without going into theology, he identifies in the rhetoric itself different types of realism, perspective, sensibility—all reflecting different cultural and anthropological presuppositions inseparable from style.[9] But if
this holds for the unit story, it holds also for a succession or cycle of such
stories. With this kind of development, recital evokes more and more
clearly a particular version of world-awareness. When one enters into the
epics of Homer or those of India, it is not only the inventory of daily life
and not only the repertoire of psychological responses that differ, but
basic apperception. This has to do with such fundamental matters as time,
orientation, causation, and reality-sense generally.

But these considerations also answer the objection that it is not meaningful thus to confront modern *fiction* with biblical *history*. I could argue
that fiction and history always encroach on each other and in any case
have a common root in what prompts to recital. But it is enough to urge
that the two kinds of rehearsal can be compared—as could two kinds of
history or two kinds of fiction—at the level of their respective realism,
perspective, sensibility, apperception, and so forth, all having their bearing
upon style and rhetoric. Auerbach's basic comparisons are between the
Odyssey and Genesis, on the one hand, and Petronius and the Gospel of
Mark on the other. The fact that the pagan texts are fictional (epic and
romance, respectively) while the biblical texts are quasi-historical is of no
significance for his study of realism.

In this context, then, we may anticipate and state our thesis. Since we
are now concerned first of all with the arts of narration, we push our
search for criteria back behind the New Testament narrative to the Old,
and make our appeal to the Hebrew anthropology, the biblical humanism,
and venture our assessment from that basis. In Israel, an earthy kind of
realism came to birth such that its recitals encompass and interweave the
whole story of heaven and earth and of man in unique fashion. If we
speak of "epiphany" today in connection with those revelations that lie at
the origin of religion or technically, as a feature of modern fiction and
lyric, Israel's "epiphany" was of such a kind that it had to be historized.
Man was seen as a responsible actor in a world-story. Man's multidimensional nature is in view, and a real world-theater, and all in an ultimate context. This world-apperception, moreover, carries with it a dra-

---

9. *Mimesis* (Princeton N.J., Princeton University Press, 1953), chaps. 1–2. For
example: "But even the human beings in the biblical stories have greater depths of
time, fate and consciousness than do the human beings in Homer; . . . their thoughts
and feelings have more layers, are more entangled" (p. 12).

matic element: The order in question is always threatened by anarchy, as the reality established is threatened by fantasy and false images, or "vain imaginations." Man is secured against these by fidelity to the revealed pattern or covenant which encompasses not only his "spiritual" faculties, but also his social and somatic existence.

The biblical narrative perpetuates this epiphany and its vicissitudes and communicates its import. Indeed, the biblical epos remains as a kind of cable or lifeline across the abysses of time and cultures, because man is here sustained over against anarchy, nonbeing, and nescience. In this sense, language is, indeed, a "house of being."

Other great cultural epiphanies or faiths have created their own ordering structures and rhetorics, testifying in various ways to particular endowments of our common human nature. But they differ in this matter of holism, in the realism and scope of their fabulation. In Israel, we are confronted with a veritable mutation, to use a secular equivalent for "election." It is not surprising that its story of man engages his social sense and channels the vitalities of his biological inheritance towards personal fulfillment and viable community.[10] Is it not the continued story of Israel, whether in the synagogue or the church, which, until recently in any case, has given history its substance, though of course this historical fabric of reality has both its visible and latent continuities?

To put it in another way, we can say that the ancient patterns of rehearsal in the Bible—these genealogies of heaven and earth, these paradigms of the human family, these vicissitudes of a pilgrim people through ancient economies, these records of conscience in the making, these annals of man's generic passions, his wrestlings with the angel, the pride and miscarriage of his works and many inventions—we can say that these ancient rehearsals may be recognized in some sort as the archetypal molds of our own histories and fabulations. In these tracks our own courses are run. Here we of the West find the world-old syndrome that coerces us from

10. This is not the occasion to deal with the demurrer which would acquiesce in the fateful legacy of the biblical understanding of man but would also assign it responsibility, especially at a psychological level, for various disorders associated with it (and in contrast with other faiths, particularly of the East) such as moralism, diabolism, holy-war mentality, etc. The point to make here is that the annals and ethic of any faith which truly relates itself to the dynamics of human nature and its irrational elements are bound to reflect the dramas of life against death, both private and public. It is, however, true that the language and symbolics of the tradition have often been infected and deformed in the course of their accepted engagements with the kingdoms of misrule. I have discussed the perversion of Christian imagery of sacrifice and atonement by alien motifs of masochism-sadism in "The Cross: Social Trauma or Redemption," in my book *Theology and Modern Literature* (Cambridge: Harvard University Press, 1958), pp. 93–110.

the cradle to the grave. When we come into the world, in whatever century since, we find ourselves in a mystery that has been mapped, even if we disbelieve it, and even if the ancient chart has all but faded away.[11] Nevertheless, our inmost being, our genes, carry this imprint, suggested by such formulas as "lost and found," "from slave to royalty," and by such models as those of pilgrim, servant, saint. If the biblical experience precisely as narrative carries this kind of meaning and this kind of holism, it is not farfetched to take it as a basis of Christian discrimination over against other forms of story.

Yet we face here one consideration which may seem to block this kind of assessment today. Not only is our contemporary fiction removed by millenniums from the biblical recitals in question, but by comparison it deals with a very foreshortened reality, with one in which the self is alienated from a wider context—deals largely, in fact with subjectivity (see again the epigraph to this section). Contemporary man and his accounts of himself forfeit the total perspectives of the biblical epic. We can understand this in the light of our Western fate. But this radical disparity does not invalidate our procedure. No doubt the biblical holism judges our attenuated field of concern and challenges the restriction of so much of our fiction to the dramas of the self. Yet even within these limitations of the contemporary novelist, distinctions can be made. It is a question as to whether within them he nevertheless wrestles with the limits imposed, whether he seeks to move "beyond alienation," and to repossess in some new way the wider orientation.

Though the believer must regret the very special focus of the best contemporary fiction as compared with the perspectives of the biblical epic or the literature of other periods, one consideration should give him pause. He may himself be confident in his inherited affirmations of the total meaningfulness of the world and in the bridges that he can build from his private experience to the wider context of history and ultimate reality. But he

11. Here we may cite one recent testimony, by the playwright Eugene Ionesco, all the more significant in that it is not a Jew who is writing: "I therefore believe that without the Jews, the world would be harsh and sad. What keeps us alive? The hope that some day or other, everyone will change, and everything will change and be good and beautiful. Without the Jews, we should not have this belief: we should not hope in the coming or the return of a Messiah, the saviour. We still hope, knowing that the Messiah is behind the door: we hope that he will open it one day and that the world will be flooded with joy and light. We all hope in the ideal City, that is to say we all hope that a new Jerusalem will rise up from the deserts and from death. We hope for the transfiguration of the world, and we shall hope for this as long as there are Jews. Without them, madness or crime; without them darkness." "Journal," *Encounter* (London) 31 (1968):14. The passage is dated 1967.

should ask himself whether this total grasp is actually earned and operative. We know too well how a traditional Christian idealism or pietism can
affirm all this, yet be quite blind to the real givens and costs and corollaries
of such a claim. The contemporary novelist, at his best, is wrestling with
these givens and impasses of our situation so as to make possible a genuine
repossession in new terms of the wider meaningfulness of the world. Or, to
say it in literary terms, he is seeking to tell the whole story again in such
a way that no stubborn elements need be bypassed.

The difficulty of this today, whether in life or in fiction, may be illustrated from Saul Bellow's *The Adventures of Augie March,* and I have
in view some remarks of Marcus Klein about the novel in his book *After
Alienation.*[12] Augie is speaking of "the axial lines of life, with respect to
which you must be straight," and which are "truth, love, peace, bounty,
usefulness, harmony!" which, he says, quiver right through him when
striving stops. And these, he observes, are "not imaginary stuff . . . because I bring my whole life to the test." Klein, citing this passage, goes on
to remark, however, that this is one of the moments when Augie's hopefulness becomes shrill. His whole life does not validate the perception. In
fact, "the novel is honest beyond Augie's knowing and it does not permit
him so easy an escape."[13] This instance illustrates both the difficulty today
of genuine as against cheap grace and the integrity of the artist who in his
own medium wrestles with the problem of valid perspectives. What we
look for in any narrative, ancient or modern, is that kind of dense inner
coherence which moves toward wider horizons with convincing logic.

III. THE BIBLICAL RECITAL

To clarify what is meant by the "holism" of the biblical epos, we may
begin by asking what might be called the prior question about narrative
in general. What special aspect of our human reality discloses itself in the
universal impulse to tell stories? We answer immediately: our sense of
temporality and succession. An anecdote links a before and an after; a
poem need not. But it goes deeper to say that a story posits a sense of
orientation and coherence. The story, the fable, the myth assume a context, an order of some kind. They impose a graph upon chaos or nescience.
They carve out a lighted space, a *zu-Hause,* in the darkness.

I am thinking of the primordial myth as the story that accompanied the
mimetic ritual. The intense group experience of epiphany required mean-

12. New York, 1965.
13. Ibid., p. 53.

ingful extrapolation, explanation, in the narrative. One recalls Durkheim's description of the origin of the categories, the projection of particularized space and time, the process of world-making. To tell a story is to posit a meaningful order, however fragmentary, a degree of coherence. If the novel of today tends sometimes to refuse the story aspect, to transcribe chaotic impressions rather than woven sequence, to prefer epiphany over rehearsal, then we confront a significant symptom of our situation. The only redeeming feature of such a reversal would be that neglected ranges of experience were calling for recognition, thus for the moment disqualifying our inherited patterns of coherence.

I am aware, of course, of the immense differences there can be in the kinds of coherence implicit in narration. The sagas of different peoples differ radically in the kinds of reality they posit, the range or levels of human and cosmic relationship they incorporate, the dimension of realism they represent.

In the Hebrew and Christian Scriptures, the narrative mode has extraordinary importance, and not only quantitatively. If one looks at the classics and charters of other religions or religious philosophies, the story aspect may be relatively marginal. Their sacred books often take the form rather of oracular aphorism or philosophical instruction or mystical treatise or didactic code. In the case of biblical man, language moved towards recital, and all heaven and earth came into it. The community renewed its identity by its rehearsals, and by telling the world the way of the world as its members had heard it. The fact that narrative had such a constitutive part in Israel's faith points us back to a level of profound cultural apperception. But this bears also upon the kind of narrative. We speak of its *holism*. By this we mean the scope of awareness, the multidimensional reality and realism, the inclusion of private and public, of the inner life and the social-historical, of somatic and visionary, of ethical and metaphysical.

If we look now at the narrative cycles of the Old Testament, we find one or another kind of overarching plot from beginnings to fulfillment, and, incorporated in it, a very dense portrayal of the human experience and existence in all its empirical reality. The oldest such cycle (taken up into the later Pentateuch) runs from the creation and the patriarchs through the Exodus from Egypt to the conquest of the Promised Land, all looking to the goal that the nations should be blessed through Israel's vocation. This graph of destiny is later enlarged so that its elements of myth and saga constitute the antecedents for the providential greatness of the reign of David. The *Aeneid* does something like this for the antecedents of imperial

Rome, beginning at the fall of Troy. The two epics celebrate the divine predestination, discipline, and blessing of their respective people, providing their different charts of time, thus enhancing the worth and pride of every member of the two commonwealths and lending meaning to their state rituals.

In the later Deuteronomic history, the epic of the people is again rehearsed, by means of the farewell discourses put in the mouth of Moses. Here the birth of the nation and its basic covenants are memorialized at a juncture between the great disasters to the northern and southern kingdoms. Only narrative, it seems, could serve the necessary self-understanding of Israel as the horizon opens beyond the recent apostasies and catastrophies to end with a call for the renewal of the covenant in a restored Jerusalem. The subsequent priestly narrative reshapes the total graph, now from creation to the postexilic situation, though in a less realistic key. But the historian who combined and interwove these rehearsals into the form in which we have them in the Hebrew canon today gave to his people a total epos and a total orientation which was at the same time rooted in the richest kind of realistic humanism.

What I would like to emphasize here is that the employment of the narrative mode—a combination of myth, saga, and history—provided not only orientation in the mysteries of time and existence, but therewith the structures of a human order against chaos, and of meaningfulness against unreason. The biblical epos secured life against death, being against non-being. In this sense again, language constituted a "house of being." Mythos and ethos were inseparable.

This crucial issue of human viability in the narrative appears also and especially in the bodies of law which are so deeply embedded in it. Just as the epic evokes the creation and the covenants of heaven and earth—that is, pledges of the stability of the cosmic order—over against the primeval chaos, so the laws set stern barriers and austere penalties against relapse into confusion. Characteristic for the laws is the sanction "I am the Lord your God," in fuller form "I am the Lord your God, who brought you forth from the land of Egypt to give you the land of Canaan, and to be your God" (Lev. 25:38). Thus the total narrative sanctions the commandments, evokes the self-understanding that bows to the obligation. We only recognize the full significance of this when we note that the demands so motivated reach to the fateful dividing line between creation and chaos, and between the human and the bestial. Just as the narrative represents the lifeline of survival through flood and desert and foes natural and supernatural, so the mandates that appeal to it are directed against outrage, enormities, and violations of nature. Both the narrative and the law reflect a dramatic sense of the jeopardies of the human community in existence, and this is evident in the attention given to incursions of the irrational, panics, abominations and hyperbolic penalties, bans and exterminations.[14] This defense of the human appears correspondingly in the law.

> You shall not give any of your children to devote them by fire to Molock. ... I am the Lord (Lev. 18:21).

> Everyone who curses his father or his mother shall be put to death (20:9).

> If your brother becomes poor, and cannot maintain himself with you, you shall maintain him. . . . I am the Lord your God (25:35, 38).

And so the prohibitions go on against removing landmarks, cutting down fruit trees, defrauding the laborer, giving a daughter in prostitution, falsifying weights and measures. All such orderings have their sanction in the narrative. They are more than morality. They are associated with the lifeline of human order and sanity.[15] Thus the urgency and apodictic character of the laws match the powerful realism and dynamics of the total story.

We are noting the relation of narrative in Israel to other genres. How is it with the poem? The close of Moses' farewell discourses in Deuteronomy offers us an example. He concludes his rehearsal of God's ways with Israel by an injunction to treasure up "this book of the law" (that is, with its setting in the narrative) "that it may be there as a witness before you." It is to be rehearsed in the assemblies of the people "as long as you live in the land which you are going over the Jordan to possess" (31:13). But then we read that in view of the anticipated breaking of the covenant, God says to Moses,

> Now therefore write this *song,* and teach it to the people of Israel; put it in their mouths, that this song may be a witness for me against the people of Israel . . . ; (for it will live unforgotten in the mouths of their descendants) (31:19–21).

14. Our modern outlook fails to see these elements of Scripture in context. Recently Robert Lowell, in a lecture at the Harvard Divinity School dealing with the biblical literature, registered his understandable revulsion at what he took to be the two most immoral books in the Bible, Joshua and the Apocalypse. He instanced the extermination of men, women, and children in the former, and the blood up to the horses' bridles in the latter. But we should read ancient texts in terms of their rhetorical genres and cultural settings. Moreover, it is important to recognize the basic motive behind such hyperbolic dramatizations: all such sanguinary fictions, whether in the form of history or prophetic anticipation, reflect in the contemporary modes of the imagination men's acute sense of the struggle against the encroachments of the primeval chaos and for the viability of the human.

15. Note Deut. 32:46–49: "Be careful to do all the words of this law. For it is no trifle for you, but it is your life."

So we have the song of Moses in Deuteronomy 32. This is again a recital of God's favor to Israel and of her apostasy, followed by God's eventual vindication. But it is in the lyric and dramatic mode. Thus the self-understanding of Israel and the individual Israelite, as brought home to them in the prose narrative, is quickened to another degree of immediacy and responsibility by the visionary poetic vehicle. Is not this the role of the poetry in the Hebrew Scriptures as a whole, especially of the Psalter in relation to the total narrative ground plan?

Thus we have observed that the older Hebrew epos provided a total orientation and coherence. It was group-binding and time-binding. It offered a well-lighted place to the human being and the group against the incursions of the irrational in any theater of experience. And we may add that it was this same map of existence which was taken over especially by the English and American Calvinists, and found later rehearsals in the work of Milton and Bunyan, and which has had its still later vicissitudes in American self-interpretation and literary fiction.

IV. REALISM AND COHERENCE

But we have in the storytelling of the Old Testament not only an over-arching world-plot, but also a very rich, dense portrayal of human experience. One way to identify the latter appears especially in the legends of Genesis. The fact that their origins can be assigned to archaic motifs associated with early epochs and transitions of society testifies to their realistic human substance. The usual typologies connect all such narrative lore with ancient culture-crises, tribal annals, or ethnological and cultic history. In the stories, as in the symbolic language, a hermeneutics of symbol and myth brings to light very ancient strata of human conscience and consciousness reflecting the evolution of society and the self.[16]

But I would emphasize a more immediate kind of documentation of the human phenomenon in our narratives, one which also distinguishes the biblical recital from familiar kinds of fanciful, or fabulous, or gratuitous invention. Religion in the Old Testament roots in man's primordial drives and social bonds; it wrestles with the powerful, intractable, but God-given raw materials of human nature. Why are the historical books so full of vivid and often shocking anecdotes about the elemental relationships, the a, b, c's of life, as it were: sex, family, property, vendetta, heroism? To cite what I have written elsewhere:

> It is not enough to say that here as in Homer we find a marvellous gamut of human nature portrayed. The point is rather this: the Bible recognizes

16. Paul Ricoeur, *The Symbolism of Evil* (New York: Harper & Row, 1967).

that God finds his way to us, and we to Him, through the deep primordial cravings, hungers, loyalties, bonds, suggested by these relationships of parent and child, husband, and wife, chieftain and follower.

These stories have to do with elemental relationships and natural yearnings like parental instinct, tribal and patriotic passion, hero worship and pride in skill or role, sentiments which involve our very entrails. They lay bare the roots of human vitality, the cables which carry the powerful voltage of human impulse and action, whether creative or destructive. The modern psychologist knows how important these ingredients in our make-up are. . . . The tree of Judaism has its roots in these kinds of human dynamics. The vitality and meaning of Messianic hopes and eschatological perspectives spring from these explosive forces in our nature.[17]

Now it is especially in the older stratum in the books of Samuel that this kind of holism can be seen. Here we follow the story of David's succession to Saul amid the strife of the tribes and war with the Philistines. We note the interweaving of Yahweh's overruling purpose with the raw material of human passions. Into the total web come not only dramas of intimate relationships, but the play of historical determinations. The narrator is interested in the skills and occupations of men: the smith, the musician, the wise woman, the rancher; and in the traits of men: astuteness, magnanimity, melancholia, jealousy, emulation. We get the full gamut of social rank. We get prudential strategies and sagacity, but also resorts to divination and necromancy and mimetic exorcisms when normal controls are swept away by incursions of the irrational or the horrors of pestilence and famine.

There is one feature of this narrative which again seems to me to be worth special consideration. The human actions recurrently burst the wonted course of affairs and explode, as it were, into the hyperbolic. They go over the limits of the human scale, in heroism or immolation, in ecstasy or horror. We have a sense of overflowing human virtue or prodigality or creaturely vitality, under brilliant realistic illumination, but it moves often into the order of the arcane, disclosure of the prodigious. But even such excursions beyond the normal are controlled in the history. We have controlled, frenzy, ritualized mania. The irrational dimensions of life, above or below, are mastered, but their energies are acknowledged and channeled.

We have an example here in one theater of what it is to tell the whole story; in these narratives, private drama is only rightly grasped in its public

17. *Otherworldliness and the New Testament* (New York: Harpers, 1954), pp. 32–36 (quotation abridged).

determination and social rituals in their metaphysical relationship. Suggestive of this total vitality is the blessing of Joseph in Deut. 33:13:

> And of Joseph he said,
> "Blessed by the Lord be his land,
> with the choicest gifts of heaven above,
> and of the deep that couches beneath."

What is the significance for our analysis of that great change in the structure of the biblical epic that arose with Jewish apocalyptic literature and that passed over into the New Testament narrative? We can illustrate by the difference between the Book of Ruth and the Book of Daniel. Ruth is by no means only a pastoral idyll. With its exquisite old-Israelite realism, it is part of the total Hebrew epos, linking as it does the period of the judges with the ancestry of David. Kinship patterns and marriage, rural economy and judicial practice, private poignancy and public—indeed international—relationships, are all essential ingredients in a short story which has its place in that wider history that encompasses the whole course of the world. The Book of Ruth is a signal example of how narrative provides orientation and coherence in the world, and how, for example, there is no truncation between the order of sexuality of the individual and a total context of meaning and value.

In the stories in the Book of Daniel: the lions' den, the fiery furnace, the feast of Belshazzar, but also in the mythological account of how one like a Son of man succeeded to the world-rule of the beasts representing the empires of the East—in all these we again have a marriage of heaven and earth, of historical circumstance and a transcendental scheme. But we have entered here upon a kind of narrative reality and style that merge with those of the Book of Revelation and indeed with aspects of our Gospels.

Is there a loss of realism and holism when these eschatological and surreal features of language are introduced? But there is still a plot. Narrative is still the necessary medium to convey meaning and coherence. It is true that the goal of world history is redefined. Alpha and Omega are reconceived. This calls for a revised version of the Hebrew world-story as a whole. Moreover, the storyteller and the hearers or readers now find themselves at the point of denouement, in Act Five. But the New Testament is still basically narrative. Self-understanding and community-understanding are still mediated through recital. Even the poetry in the New Testament is often, again, confessional recital. And the law of the new movement in Israel is sanctioned by the recital.

Ernst Käsemann, in an often-quoted thesis, has written that apocalyptic was the mother of theology—in the sense that the interim opened up by the portrayal of the end-time required new reflections on the meaning of the divine plan. This thesis can be formulated in literary terms: The new vision of time and the world called forth new rhetorics.[18] But the Gospels show us that recital was still the inevitable medium, and that narrative, much of it of a very earthy kind like the parables of Jesus, was required to domesticate revelation in daily life. We see here the continuing Hebraic demand that epiphany be historized. In the Gospel narrative, the realism and the holism of Hebraic man is safeguarded and no truncation is allowed between the somatic and the spiritual, between the individual and the group, or between the historical and the transcendent. The narration makes men at home in the world, even when that world has entered upon its final transformation.

V. RHETORICS OF THE HEART

A third aspect of the biblical narratives to be discussed is that of their styles. We have in mind the Old Testament material, first of all. This evidences in many ways what we find in all ancient epic, the prior *oral* stage of recital, a feature which lends it an enlivening sense of actuality. With this goes the anonymity of the speaking voice of the writer, another feature which lends prominence to the action, as though events spoke for themselves, and one which conveys the community import of what is told. Much of it has, moreover, what is common to all cult-rehearsal as distinguished from universal storytelling, aspects of formality,[19] which, at a second or third remove, reflect older cultic or ceremonial setting; in any case, features of sobriety and economy of language which are determined by the special sense of destiny associated with the tribes or the nation. No doubt one can recognize elements in Genesis or the Book of Judges or II Samuel, and so on, which go back to a quasi-secular inspiration, but these have been subsequently metamorphosed by being taken up into the more fateful context of some larger cycle. An analogy is found in the way in which an archaic war ballad and taunt-song has been transformed into what we now have in the Song of Deborah in Judges 5; a liturgical paean for use at one of the

18. See my *Early Christian Rhetoric: The Language of the Gospel* (Cambridge, Mass.: Harvard University Press, 1971), especially chap. 4, "The Story." (This edition is a reissue, with a new introduction, of *The Language of the Gospel* [New York: Harper & Row, 1964]).

19. "The prose is not the common colloquial language of everyday life, but is more artistic in its composition and has some sort of rhythmical construction." H. Gunkel, *The Legends of Genesis*, tr. W. S. Carruth (Chicago: Open Count Press, 1901), p. 38.

older Israelite sanctuaries as part of a cycle of *res gestae* or heroic rehearsals of the tribes.[20]

In recognizing the ways in which the styles of Hebrew narrative were variously colored by the cultic factor or by the special apperceptions of Israel as a people with an historical calling, I would not give the impression that we have to do with hieratic language, though the so-called priestly stratum has a special formality of this kind. We should not be misled by the way in which ideas of a sacred style have been falsely imposed on the Scriptures by later canonization and translation, and by special views of inspiration elaborated by synagogue and church. What distinguishes these histories from common storytelling, and even from comparable culture-epic, is finally the depth of motive that lies behind the utterance, the impulse behind the birth of language (behind what Ebeling and Fuchs call the *Sprach-Ereignis* or *Wort-Geschehen*), the urgency of the fabulation, all of which shape the narrative in the single episode and in the sequences.[21] I have spoken of this dynamic aspect of the narrative earlier in this chapter in another way in saying that it was a special feature of Israel's epiphanies that they required historization.

But there are more specific features of style that can be identified. With respect to the Hebrew language itself, the prominence of the verb commands first attention, as well as the plastic and sensuous character of the vocabulary. In both respects, abstraction is largely still beyond the horizon. Syntax is paratactic, and clause is added to clause with the simplest construction. This is what Gertrude Stein has in mind when she writes that "really in the Old Testament there is no sentence existing and no paragraphing." Her point is that the real import of the telling goes beyond conventional interest in the one-dimensional succession of events.[22] Gunkel, commenting on the paratactic feature, associates it with the tenseness "of the connection of the successive clauses, and attributes it to the undeviating energy of the narrator."[23] Yet while in one dimension experience is ordered

---

20. J. Blenkinsopp, "Ballad Style and Psalm Style in the Song of Deborah," *Biblica* 42 (1961): 61–76. Cited in my *Early Christian Rhetoric*, p. 97. Another analogy is the way in which the old English ballads were transformed in the course of the Christianizing of the culture. Cf. M. Jarret-Kerr, *Studies in Literature and Belief* (London: Rockliff, n.d.), chap. 2.

21. "Each successive member is linked to the preceding one, . . . each preceding member appears as the natural cause or at least the antecedent of the succeeding one. . . . These narratives, then, are tense in their connection. The narrators do not like digressions, but press with all their energy toward the mark." Gunkel, *Legends*, p. 70.

22. *Narrative: Four Lectures*, p. 19. With respect to the rarity of the period in Beckett's later fiction, Hugh Kenner writes: "No sequence of sentences can approxi-

in teleological succession, its reality is also evoked in another dimension, which we may call the *dialogic*. Style, in this respect, is not a matter of Hebrew syntax so much as one of the special sensibility and psychology of this people. Israel construed its world very much in terms of relationships, encounter, address and response, the confrontation of wills. Events and episodes have their import in this domain, in the aspect of transaction. It is not surprising, therefore, that the narrative style of Hebrew narrative is short on description and foregoes detailed portrayal and unbroken sequence of events. Reality is not here, but at the level of personal and community response. With some oversimplification it has been claimed that Israel's genius is associated with the ear, as that of other cultures and their epics is with the eye. In any case, the "word" was evidently primary for the Hebrew religious experience, "word" not in the sense of language in general, but in the sense of the word of address and of dialogue.

It follows that the subjective experience of the actors in the narratives is not the chief subject and is conveyed chiefly by their action, deportment, and external indications, as well as by their speech.

> The ancient storyteller does not share the modern point of view that the most interesting and worthy theme for art is the soul-life of man; his childlike taste is fondest of the outward, objective facts. . . . He has an extraordinary capacity for selecting just the action which is most characteristic for the state of feeling of his hero. . . . Little as these primitive men could talk about their soul-life, we gain the impression that they are letting us look into the very hearts of their heroes.[24]

Gunkel is speaking here of the legends of Genesis, but the characterization applies more generally.

There is one other feature of the Hebrew language and syntax which is consonant with all that has been said, and this is the minor role of the adjective. But this is only one of the more striking indices of the absence in biblical narrative of elements familiar in other forms of saga and epic: circumstantial description; personal portraiture; detailed, sensuous delineation. In these respects the Hebrew histories, while they evoke an abundant and many-levelled humanity, nevertheless focus on actions, relationships, and their moral nexus. It follows, as Auerbach has shown, that the Hebrew narrative styles lack the unbroken surface continuity and pictorial

---

mate the ultimate statement The Unnamable yearns to make, since every sentence must begin somewhere and end somewhere else (*abitus, transitus, aditus,* wrote Geulincx) and no choice of a beginning or an ending can fail to exclude a thousand others." *Samuel Beckett* (New York, 1961), p. 188.

23. Cf. n. 21 above.

24. Gunkel, *Legends,* pp. 61–62.

fullness of Homer. The continuity and the reality-sense lie deeper, and are conveyed by a seemingly less developed gamut of language, but by one well adapted to the dramatic transactions of the heart. We shall note at a later point certain analogies between this observation and some of the more recent explorations in modern fiction.

VI. PARABLES AND
THE DEEPER ENIGMA OF MAN

With these interrelated aspects of the biblical epos before us—world-plot, concreteness, and style—we propose now to single out fundamental features of the biblical storytelling which might still fairly be used as tests of, or as foil to, modern narrative. After two millenniums and more, we are not so foolish as to take biblical narrative as a model in any narrow sense, least of all in its ideology. In order to make a relevant literary comparison, we must go deeper.

One such challenge has to do with the motive for narration. This raises a question which is so elementary it is often not even thought of: Why narrative at all! Why does narrative exist at all in the old Hebrew society and why, in any case, so much of it? Or, again, what prompts the modern fabulist? For what good reason are novels written in the first place? This is a good question, because it points us back to what should be the profound life-relationship of this genre or mode of language. And it points us to the elemental compulsion which called forth precisely narration as a form of awareness among the early Hebrews, and determined the scope and realism of the recitals that followed. But this factor is connected with their survival power.

There is one basic test of all storytelling, which again we are apt to forget, and that is that it should hold the auditor or reader. So the reader says, "I could not put it down," or, "I had to see how it came out." This feature of any extended narration points to something much deeper than contrivance. The act of telling must spring from a profound necessity. There must be an initial urgency, life-force, in the storyteller, an *Erzählerfreude,* that lends power like that of a spell to his fabulation, and enables him to order experience in persuasive designs. One of the most illuminating things ever said about a fabulist, and it was said about Ezra Pound, was that he provided humanity with incentives to *go on living*. I would put this beside that primordial secret of a narration which induces the reader to *go on reading*. This is not a truism. There are many stories which are not read or heard to the end. The world they create does not come into existence. It is not real enough. The biblical epos has continued to be read, and the world it created has continued to be real for men of many kindreds and generations down to the present time. It has "held" the world in more senses than one. This first test, then, is a challenge to the ultimate springs of motivation of the novelist.

No doubt there is abundant justification for many of the less ambitious kinds of fiction which are written or told in all periods. But our concern here is with the ultimate criteria of the genre, and therefore with its most important contemporary examples or directions.

A second test is that of what we have called holism. In the biblical narration, no significant dimensions are scanted. The private and the public are interrelated, the psychological and the social, the empirical and the metaphysical. And there is a robust reality-sense, a power in being, and it is related to the fact that man in Scripture, precisely in his total perspectives, is still linked with the archaic hidden roots and fibers of his prehistoric and biological inheritance. This test is a challenge to any kind of truncation of man, whether naturalistic or spiritualizing or solipsist. It exposes particularly one dominant feature of modern letters, that which can be generally characterized as the "epiphany." For the epiphanic moment in modern experience and the modern novel, which often has to carry the whole burden of meaning, represents a highly fragmentary grasp of reality. The momentary vision in question may have a romanticist, an existentialist, or a surrealist character, but in whatever form, it evidences a forfeiture of relationships, and so of holism. It testifies, indeed, to an impoverishment of vitality in the visionary, rather than the contrary. For when epiphany is powerful, it orders reality.

It is to be acknowledged that the imagination of our time meets all but insuperable obstacles in its tasks of ordering our confusions. In this dilemma it is more courageous for the artist to explore what authentic contacts with reality open up for him than to cling to structures and idioms that have lost their authority. Yet the impulse to "tell more," if not to "tell all," is ever present in modern letters, as indeed is testified by recurrent wrestlings with ancient epic, including the Bible, and by transformations of the novel genre to bring it closer to the full range of experience, new and old.

There is one further challenge presented by the biblical epos. It is difficult to state it without seeming to involve theology. We have already had it in view when discussing the "dialogic" dimension of that narrative. The question raised is that of doing justice to the full mystery of the self and its aliveness at the level of interpersonal encounter and mutuality. The unique humanism of the Old Testament would appear to rest upon some momentous cultural drama that moved the race along towards the personal.

Its narrative, therefore, evokes something more than the usual suspense-
ful turns of fortune of men and societies, and something more than the joys
and sorrows, hopes and disappointments of life. In such classic epic and
fictions, the deeper enigma of man is hardly touched. What is missing is
some sense of that secret of his being where he is a mixture of freedom
and helplessness, of loneliness and entanglement, and where all this carries
with it a consciousness of responsibility, and where man is sensitive not
only to external approval or disapproval, but to internal peace or shame.
It is a question of the dramas of the heart, and of the share of men's willing
and choosing in the fatefulness of the world.[25]

I can do no better to suggest this special awakening of the self than by
noting how in the biblical episodes, in the Old Testament stories, God, as
it were, looks man in the eye. This intense facet of awareness may be
evoked for us if we remember occasions when our parents, desiring to
track something down, bade us look them in the eye. "Eyeball to eyeball,"
we say. This kind of naked confrontation and searching of the human self
can mean a calling to account. We think of Jesus looking at Peter after his
denial. (Auerbach chooses this as an example of a new kind of realism in
the ancient world; a banal police-court incident linked with world significance.) Or we think of Nathan's words to David: "Thou art the man!" The
kiss of Judas suggests this order of personal existence, or the handwriting
on the wall in Daniel. But such moral reverberations of a positive character can also be evoked in the narrative: Joseph disclosing himself to his
brothers, or the mutual magnanimity of David and the three mighty men
who, at the risk of their lives, brought him water from the well which was
by the gate of Bethlehem, to solace him at a moment of homesickness and
dereliction. Quite apart from theology, all this represents a deeper kind of
humanism, an existential kind of realism, such that the narrative pierces to
the heart's core of the reader and binds us hand and foot. This test exposes
a great deal of fiction, past and present, particularly today much that is
inspired by a subpersonal aestheticism or an affective pathos, whether
athletic or sophisticated, or the novel of ideas, all of which bypass this
dimension. On the other hand, it is here that justice should be done to a
Salinger who has the delicate registers to deal with the infinitely subtle and
complex world of relationships at this level.

The dimension of involvement of which we have been speaking refers
first of all to the characters in the given narrative. But the reader is also
involved. We are reminded of Berthold Brecht, therefore. For if it was his
view that there must be a distance between the audience and the action, it

25. See chap. 2.

was to ensure that the spectator's responsibility was demanded. Transferred to the arts of narration, this means that the hearer or reader should not be a victim of hypnotic compulsion or sorcery. Brecht spoke significantly, therefore, of a dialectical or epic theater. The biblical epic has this character. It is not seductive, subjective, romantic. It does not work by a depersonalizing enchantment. When one finds sentiment in the Old Testament— as, for example, in the sacrifice of Isaac or the immolation of Jephthah's daughter—any evasion into common pathos is blocked by a high art of austerity, or any consent to disguised forms of masochism or sadism such as are invited in current novels and plays. The sufferer in such episodes is not a victim, but an actor at a sacrifice.[26]

One could speak of this added dimension of narrative as that of intentionality. If a novelist is to "tell the whole story," it is not enough that we should have a richly circumstantialized account of all that happened, even if it includes many levels of experience. Added to all such objectives, there should be the baffling dimension of intentionality, ultimate freedom, personal reality in its movement. What is in view here is well suggested in remarks of Gertrude Stein:

> Everybody's life is full of stories: your life is full of stories; my life is full of stories. They are very occupying, but they are not really interesting. What is interesting is the way everyone tells their stories; [and at the same time she was listening to the tellers' revelation of their "basic nature."] If you listen, really listen, you will hear people repeating themselves. You will hear their pleading nature or their attacking nature or their asserting nature.[27]

Miss Stein could speak of this as catching the "rhythm of personality." But if this dimension of personal reality is in the novel, it will also involve the reader and his core of freedom.[28]

---

26. Quoting Robert Frost, "A Masque of Reason" in *Complete Poems of Robert Frost* (New York: Henry Holt, 1949), p. 596. God explains to Job why he had caused him to suffer:

> Society can never think things out:
> It has to see them acted out by actors,
> Devoted actors at a sacrifice.

27. As quoted (with added comment) in the introduction by T. H. Wilder to Gertrude Stein's *Four Americans* (New Haven, 1947), p. x.

28. "What Robbe-Grillet is after (and to a greater or lesser degree his colleagues in the form . . .) is not simply 'objectification of things,' but the forced inclusion of the reader in the process of inventing art, inventing stories, inventing experience. . . . It is a view that shows Robbe-Grillet, the chief propagandist of the nouveau roman, to be as stern a moralist as he is a rationalist. . . . All of [his novels] do succeed in some degree in scattering one's preconceptions and thereby making one aware of the possibilities of a re-energized involvement on the reader's part in the invention of art and life." Eliot Fremont-Smith, reviewing *La Maison de rendez-vous* in the *New York Times,* Nov. 23, 1966.

We find an echo of this dissatisfaction with mere stories today and a demand for that kind of personal dimension we have found in the biblical narrative in Samuel Beckett's play for radio, *Embers*.[29] Henry exclaims:

> Stories, stories, years and years of stories, till the need came to me, for someone, to be with me, anyone, a stranger, to talk to, imagine he hears me, years of that, and then, now, for someone who . . . knew me, in the old days, anyone, to be with me, imagine he hears me, what I am, now.[30]

What Henry craves is not "stories," but a voice. And here Henry and Beckett himself speak for an epoch, as Hugh Kenner suggests. For as to the "stories": "That is where the Newtonian universe belongs also: It was a story Europe told itself for many decades."[31] In *Embers* the character Bolton, in a climax of tremendous poignancy, pleads for "response, personal impingement as against mechanism," in asking mutely "for whatever cannot be specified, for whatever communion looks out of another's eyes."[32]

We have before us, then, these observations on the biblical epos and the literary tests it offers to modern narrative. We find the modern novel lacking in this kind of holism or total humanism. This is, first of all, a literary observation. We are not complaining that modern fiction does not present the biblical world view or theology. We are saying that its humanism is partial or selective, narrowly focused, for example, upon the dramas of the modern self. Or, if wider contexts are implicit, they are not integrally related, say the public world or the metaphysical. We know that there are good reasons for this. Nevertheless, a theological criticism must register this fact, and at a literary level. So Georg Lukacs can make an analogous literary criticism, though writing as a Marxist. Speaking of the dominance of *Angst* and alienation in modern fiction, he says that the test is whether the writer's view is able to include—or, better, demands—a dynamic, complex analytical rendering of social relationships or whether it leads to loss of perspective and historicity."[33] A theological criticism can also make the same diagnosis and demand.

Even when a novelist seeks to incorporate metaphysical relationships into his work, we can often observe that the procedure is not structurally persuasive. In one form it has the effect of an unconvincing *deus ex machina.* Thus in *Les Faux-Monnayeur,* at the point of Bernard's deepest despair, André Gide introduces an angel of comfort to strengthen the youth in a vision. The passage is moving, but has an aura of the romantic and the

---

29. *Krapp's Last Tape and Embers* (London, 1959).
30. Ibid., pp. 24–25.
31. *Samuel Beckett,* p. 184.
32. Ibid., p. 186.
33. *Realism in Our Time* (New York), p. 82.

staged. Miracles in our time are difficult to bring off. In another form, presentation of the metaphysical dimension is only effected at the expense of all others. In his *Reprieve,* Sartre's hero Mathieu, caught up in the mobilization on the eve of World War II, has an apocalyptic vision of the total devastation not only of Paris but of the world, an eschatological epiphany that confers on him an inhuman liberation of the self. This leap beyond all involvement of the person is determined by Sartre's view of freedom and is unpersuasive if we step outside the ideology which controls his fiction and drama.[34]

In all such cases, the gulf between empirical and transcendental is not genuinely bridged. We have observed the same hiatus in the case of Augie March's "axial lines" in Bellow's novel. Our criticism will vary with particular novelists and works. For example, a case like that of James Baldwin's *Go Tell It On the Mountain* is particularly interesting, because the metaphysical dimension is evoked in biblical categories. A powerful searchlight is beamed upon patterns of human relationship and transactions in the heart, viewed in their ultimate religious reference. In these dramas of soul-saving, whose syndrome has been established by a long history of introvert piety in America, Baldwin's focus on subjectivity is dictated by his material. It is to his credit that he attempts to relate this claustral dimension of religion to wider moral and social realities. Yet one remains dissatisfied with the novel because of recurrent features of haziness and conventionality in the characterizations and the language. What is missing becomes clearer if one recalls the way in which Faulkner handles analogous material in *The Sound and the Fury.* Another successful attempt to deal with Christian supernaturalism in terms of our modest sensibility is Frederick Buechner's novel, *The Final Beast.*[35]

All in all, it is to be recognized that the modern novelist has to work within the givens of his epoch. We cannot ask him to be a Cervantes or a Tolstoi. The engagement with subjectivity and alienation has fallen to him as by a kind of fate. This situation has perforce narrowed and reduced the field of observation, and has located the struggle for orientation and meaning in the self and its dramas, thereby, for the time being, placing in question all wider contexts and the more total perspectives of the past. Amid

34. Proust, in *Albertine disparve,* offers a very much more persuasive parallel to Sartre. Marcel, in Venice, sees the whole city disintegrate before his eyes as an aspect of his moral anguish in allowing his mother to leave without him. Terrified by a sense of irrevocable solitude, all reality outside him becomes empty and devastated, and Venice is dissolved as his will is paralyzed.

35. New York: Athenaeum, 1965. Cf. also Jerome Nilssen, *The Drowning and the Dancing* (Philadelphia: Fortress Press, 1967).

the relativities and disarray consequent on a long history of necessary eman-
cipations, he seeks the final ground of things. In literary terms, this means
that language must be kept close to all vicissitudes of his experience. Yet
in the ultimate urgency of speech and of marrying the word to a changing
reality, the narrator may still find himself obscurely prompted by the profound categories and voices of the world-story of the Scriptures.

2

Scenarios of Life
and Destiny

Brief and concise utterances fell from Him, for He was no
sophist, but His Word was the power of God.

Justin, *Apology*

I. FIGURATIONS OF THE SECULAR

Among the narrative elements in the New Testament, we now turn to the
parables of Jesus. That storytelling had such a central place in the very
beginning of the Gospel means more than may at first appear. It is not
enough to say that Jesus used the form of the parable only as a good
pedagogical strategy. It was not merely to hold the attention of his hearers
that he told stories or took good illustrations out of his file. There was
something in the nature of the case that evoked this rhetoric, something
in the nature of the Gospel. At the very least, there is the assumption that
action is significant, and that the varied activities, pursuits, and vocations
of men's life in nature are fateful.

Here we are reminded again that art forms in any age are connected
with basic assumptions about existence. The forms of literature in any
society are governed, if not by theology, at least by world-attitudes of one
kind or another. In the case of Jesus and his hearers, the unconscious
assumption is, further, that all life has the character of a story and of a plot.
This world-story has many characters in it; this overall plot has many sub-
plots or episodes, each of which reflects the significance of the whole. The
new speech of Jesus carries this Jewish outlook to a new stage: The
denouement of the world-story is come; the characters and their little histories are now in Act V; in fact, we hear twelve o'clock beginning to strike.

Antecedents of the parable, or *mashal,* before Jesus used it are found in
the Old Testament, in the intertestamental and apocalyptic writings, and

71

especially in the sayings of the rabbis. The term meant, first of all, a comparison of some kind, but it included a wide variety of metaphors, similitudes, riddles, mysteries, and illustrations. Many of these were brief tropes, and we find such on Jesus' lips, as when he speaks of the "salt of the earth," or quotes, "Physician, heal thyself." But many of the Jewish parables have a narrative character, as do many of those in the Gospels. Even here we find varieties. Some of the parables appear to be straight narratives about a given individual case, ending with an application: the good Samaritan, the rich fool; or somet'mes about more than one person, as, for example, the Pharisee and the publican. These have been called "example-stories," in the sense that the hearer should go and do likewise, or take warning by the given example. But we have learned to avoid this classification. There is more to such parables than any such flat moral application. In the parable of the lost sheep, in any case, the upshot is not that one should or should not go and do likewise. We have, rather, an extended image—the shepherd's retrieval of the lost sheep and his joy—a narrative image which reveals, rather than exemplifies.

It is this revelatory character of Jesus' parables which is to be stressed.[1] Here Jesus is in line with the prophets and the apocalyptists as one who uses tropes or extended images to unveil mysteries, but above all to mediate reality and life. This is particularly clear in the so-called parables of the Kingdom, like those of the sower and the mustard seed, in which Jesus mediates his own vision and his own faith. This understanding of Jesus' figures of speech is supported by our modern discussion of the metaphor in literary criticism. A simile sets one thing over against another; the less known is clarified by that which is better known. But in the metaphor we have an image with a certain shock to the imagination, which directly conveys vision of what is signified.[2]

Yet we find also, of course, teaching parables and polemic parables, like those of the prodigal son or the workers in the vineyard, in which the revelatory image is employed to justify and defend Jesus' mission against misunderstanding or attack. The larger observation is that Jesus uses fig-

1. "Thus the Christ preaching in parables appears as one who reveals mysteries, and not as one who instructs the multitudes"—M. Hermaniuk, *La Parabole évangélique* (Louvain: 1947), pp. 287–88. The same point is well stated by Günther Bornkamm: "The parables are the preaching itself." (*Jesus of Nazareth*, tr. Irene and Fraser McLuskey with James M. Robinson [New York: Harpers, 1960], p. 69.)

2. Even when Jesus' parables of the Kingdom are introduced by such a phrase as "the Kingdom of Heaven is like," we do not have true similes. It is generally recognized today that such introductory phrases only mean: The following story bears upon some aspect of the Kingdom. The parable of the sower, for example, is a developed image and a revealing metaphor, not an instructive simile or allegory.

ures of speech in an immense number of ways. The variety of the parables is only one aspect of this variety. As Hermaniuk observes, "By contrast with the rabbinic *meshalim,* the parables of Jesus are largely free of rigid and stereotyped formulas. They move with a great deal of freedom and are not constrained by any 'rule of the schools'."[3] The use of narrative for purposes of comparison and analogy is found in full creative flexibility in Jesus' usage. Indeed, we may say that the term *parable* is misleading, since it suggests a single pattern and often distorts our understanding of this or that special case.

For our purposes, what is of special interest in the parables of Jesus is not only that he told stories, but that these stories are so human and realistic. One can even speak of their secularity. The persons in question, the scenes, the actions are not usually "religious." It is true that Riesenfeld and others have urged that there is a large element of quasi-allegorical religious reference to Old Testament themes in the parables in such allusions as those to the king, the shepherd, the vineyard, the feast, the harvest, the act of sowing, and so forth.[4] On this view, Jesus is not just evoking everyday human experience, but is bringing in familiar images drawn from the ancient piety of Israel. This feature should not be exaggerated. We should not be so rigid as to exclude all such overtones. But the impact of the parables lay in their immediate, realistic authenticity. In the parable of the lost sheep, the shepherd is an actual shepherd, and not a flash-back to God as the shepherd of Israel or to the hoped-for Messiah who will shepherd Israel. To press these images in this way is to pull the stories out of shape and to weaken their thrust. In view, indeed, of the entire freedom with which Jesus uses pictures and comparisons, we can believe that he may in one case or another exploit such connotations. But this is exceptional. Where such allegorization of the parables appears, moreover, we can often recognize the hand of the later editors.

3. *La Parabole,* p. 194. Full justice to the rabbinic parables requires that we recognize their occasional prophetic and noncasuistic character. It is not enough to say with Bornkamm "The rabbis also relate parables in abundance, to clarify a point in their teaching and explain the sense of a written passage, but always as an aid to the teaching and an instrument in the exegesis of an authoritatively prescribed text" (*op cit*). One can point to rabbinic parables which have, as it were, a kerygmatic character and stand apart from exegesis of the law; see especially the words ascribed to ben Zacchai on his deathbed, Berakoth 28b; Pirke Aboth 3:17; and Shabbath 153a, the banquet parable.

4. H. Riesenfeld, "The Parables in the Synoptic and the Johannine Traditions," *Svensk Exegetisk Årsbok* 25 (1960): 37–61. (Also in *The Gospel Tradition: Essays by Harald Riesenfeld,* tr. Margaret Rowley [Philadelphia: Fortress Press, 1970], pp. 139–169). See also E. C. Hoskyns and N. Davey, *The Riddle of the New Testament* (New York, 1931), pp. 177–91.

In the realism and the actuality of the parables we recognize Jesus the layman. It is not only human life that is observed, but nature as well, or man in nature. This realism, moreover, has to do with things going on. This is a world in which, as a matter of course, things happen, men and women do things, one thing leads to another. And all this living is real and significant. The incidents may have some exceptional feature (for example, the three measures of meal in the parable of the leaven: "enough to provide a meal for 162 persons," Dalman); or they may fix upon some critical life situation (thus the unfaithful servant at the point of exposure); but they do have authentic verisimilitude.

It can be said, indeed, that this whole aspect of the parables, their naturalness and secularity, is only one side of them. There is also the application that Jesus gives to them, and that is moral and religious. But, nevertheless, we insist that these sharply focused snapshots of life do reveal something very important about the storyteller himself and about the Gospel, apart from their further bearing.

Jesus, without saying so, by his very way of presenting man, shows that for him man's destiny is at stake in his ordinary creaturely existence— domestic, economic, and social. This is the way God made him. The world is real. Time is real. Man is a toiler and an "acter" and a chooser. The parables give us this kind of humanness and actuality. There is no romance or idealization here, no false mysticism, and no miracles, no impulse towards escape into fantasy or into sentimentality. We have stories, indeed, but they stay close to things as they are.

Now, of course, Jesus' thought moves on beyond the actual stories. They are only springboards or doors to something more important. There is the picture side of the parable, and there is the meaning or application. "Go and do likewise." Or, "Pay the price." Or, "Trust in the harvest." But there is no great leap out of the world here. The grace of the Gospel is just as "down to earth" as is the father's treatment of the prodigal son. The second chance which is opened up for God's people is just as definite as that offered to the barren fig tree. And so in the other cases. We speak of Jesus' vivid parables and his skill in teaching. This is not to say enough. Jesus is not merely clarifying difficult ideas. He is leading men to make a judgment and to come to a decision. The stories are so told as to compel men to see things as they are, by analogy indeed. Sluggish or dormant awareness and conscience are thus aroused. The parables make men give attention, come alive, and face things. And they do this by evoking men's everyday experience. It is implicit that a man can be saved where he is.

And, indeed, the Gospel proposes not to substitute another world for this one, but to redeem and to transfigure the present world.

All this has been well said by Ernst Fuchs:

> Without question, it is from within this sphere of community and family living that Jesus speaks. It is from this life that he takes illustrations for his parables. We see men going about the streets and knocking at windows, we hear the sounds of their feasts; the peasant goes into the field, sows and reaps; the wife occupies herself with the small stretch of ground behind the house. We recognize the rich and the poor, the respected man and the scoundrel, gaiety and distress, sorrow and thanksgiving. But all that is not just scenery, not just "material" for a poet. . . . Jesus is not just using the details of this world as a springboard (*Anknuepfungspunkt*), but means precisely this "world." . . . Jesus calls for faith and therefore decision. This decision places the man who responds on the side of God and the marvellous divine work in hand (Matt. 17.20). But: What the hearer now does, he does in the same area of daily life that Jesus evokes so vividly and plastically in his sayings and parables![5]

There is another way to come at the parables. Men in all kinds of societies and religions tell stories, and tell them for their lessons. We shall agree, moreover, that there is nothing unique about the vividness and concreteness with which human life is struck off in Jesus' parables. We can find this in Homer, in the decorations of ancient Egyptian tombs, and elsewhere. But there is a great deal of difference as to the depth or superficiality with which man is presented. As we have noted in our preceding chapter, some good stories turn upon the fortunes of men and women, the ups and downs of life. The appeal of such stories and such wisdom as they have is identified especially with the plot and its surprises. Other good stories turn on the perennially interesting topic of character in men, their varying traits and types, and the consequence of these. Or a good story may have its chief appeal in the sheer surface delineation, the absorbing detail and concreteness of the portrayal.

In none of such fictions, however, do we necessarily have man and the enigma of man adequately presented. What may be missing, as we have indicated in that earlier context, is some sense of that secret of his being where he is a mixture of freedom and helplessness, of responsibility and entanglement, and where he is sensitive not only to external approval or disapproval, but to internal peace or shame.

5. "Das Neue Testament und das hermeneutische Problem," *Zeitschrift für Theologie und Kirche* 58 (1961): 211.

The difference between various levels of fiction and the special Christian contribution is recognized in an authoritative way by André Gide in a passage in *Les Faux-Monnayeurs*:

> It seems to me that one kind of tragic dimension has for the most part been missing in literature up until now. The novel has concerned itself with the strokes of fate, with good and bad fortune, with social inter-changes, with the conflict of passions, with characters, but not at all with the essence of the human being.
>
> To carry the drama over to the moral plane—this, however, was the task of Christianity. Yet properly speaking, there is no such thing as a Christian novel. There are those which aim at edification, but that is not at all what I have in mind. It is a question of moral tragedy—of that kind which makes so momentous the text: "If salt has lost its taste, how can its saltness be restored?" It is this kind of tragedy which concerns me.[6]

It is also to the point here to quote the great classicist Wilamowitz, speaking of men as they appear in Homer. He observes,

> They charm us like children of Goethe's "Prometheus": a race born to suffer and weep, to enjoy and be glad—and not to take account of good and bad, or of guilt and destiny, as the case is similarly with their blessed kindred, the gods.[7]

Of course, in the Greek tragedies we get another kind of story, and the mystery of man is profoundly stated by Aeschylus and Sophocles, as well as a sense of overruling justice. Without going into comparisons, we can say that in the parables of Jesus men come before us in their moral mystery and in a perspective of divine severity and love. But what is *sui generis* is the way in which these deeper dimensions are married to such ordinariness and secularity. The deepest mysteries of providence and destiny are at home with this naturalness. Here we have in Jesus' sayings the counterpart of his own person and presence among men: not as a philosopher, priest, or scribe, but as an artisan; not in the desert or in the temple, but in the marketplace.

All this bears, too, on the style of the parables. Precise observation, actuality of presentation, art beyond art in the telling. One can compare Jesus' parables in the matter of form with those of the rabbis. One can note the particular twists given them by the evangelists or in such later versions as we find in the Gospel of Thomas or in the church fathers. The rabbinic

---

6. Paris: Gallimard, 1925, p. 160.

7. Introduction to the *Agamemnon of Aeschylus,* cited by G. Bornkamm, *Das Ende des Gesetzes* (Munich: Chr. Kaiser Verlag, 1952), p. 173.

parables are often beyond praise for their purpose. But as Joachim Jeremias writes, those in our Synoptic Gospels "reveal a definite personal style, a singular clarity and simplicity, a matchless mastery of construction."[8]

This formal uniqueness is related to the urgency of Jesus' errand. The rabbis can use the parable in illustration of a wide variety of topics, and often, therefore, with less sense of import and more expansiveness or colorfulness (also in interpretive supplement) and more tendency toward allegory. The parables of Jesus, in addition to their revelatory character, are shaped more consistently towards a direct personal appeal or challenge, and their sobriety of style and sharpness of focus serve well the fatefulness of the issue in view. We can recognize this even if we disregard such introductions as "Listen!" or such conclusions as "He that hath ears to hear, let him hear!"

We cannot but be surprised by the fact that such incomparable human and naturalistic, and artistic portrayal of human life should come to us from one who spoke out of an acute eschatological crisis. Jesus saw men on the brink of world-judgment and transformation. Yet we have in the parables no stridency and no fanaticism. Must one not say that it was the very intensity of his world-dissolving vocation which accounts for the consummate shape of these sayings, these crystals of human language? His revolutionary role and message had its high-pitched aspects and accents, but these never took the form of shrillness, of the esoteric or the angelic. The one feature of his parables which echoes his eschatological challenge is the trait of hyperbole, which often appears here as in his teaching generally. This is the only point at which they appear to diverge from realism, and yet only in such a way as to suggest the element of surprise or contrast in the situation.

II. REVELATORY IDIOMS

To know who Jesus was, it is not enough to ask what he said about himself or his mission. In his modes of speech we may recognize yet another clue to the mystery of his being. In certain ages of culture we know how earlier artistic forms, whether in painting or music or poetry, come to a moment of perfection in some great master. He is able both to exploit all the initiatives of his predecessors and at the same time to relate himself and the forms he employs to a new occasion. So in Jesus, it is as though many ancient tributaries of speech, many styles, merged in him. The dis-

8. *The Parables of Jesus,* 2nd rev. ed., tr. S. H. Hooke (New York: Scribners, 1972), p. 12.

course of prophet, lawgiver, and wise man meet in him. He unites in himself many roles.

The most obvious reconciliation of opposites or of differences here is that of the wise man and the seer. We find at home in his speech the parable of the wisdom tradition, as well as the prophetic oracle. Jesus' indebtedness to the wisdom tradition of his people is evident not only in the parable form which he uses, but also in his aphorisms, which he uses in a variety of sophisticated forms.

On the other hand, his indebtedness to the prophetic tradition appears in a variety of ways. The prophet is the spokesman of the potent and dynamic word, the word that acts. For a right understanding of this kind of utterance, we can go to simpler cultures where men recognize the mystery of language. In the Old Testament we see the quasi-magical power of the blessing and the curse, the promise and the woe, the ban and the name-giving. In Jesus' speech, this depth of the word reappears. His beatitudes are not sentimental congratulations, but, like the woes that accompany them, oracular exclamations. The seven beatitudes in the Book of Revelation illuminate their character and context. Jesus' prophetic-eschatological pronouncements are loaded with dynamite, and represent the ethicizing and the spiritualizing of the ancient tradition of the spell, the charm, and the magic command.

Yet Jesus himself is neither sage nor apocalyptist, though he uses both traditions. In a sovereign way he transforms and reconciles these different rhetorics and, we can add, the tradition of lawgiver. We recall the saying of Jeremiah: "The law shall not perish from the priest, nor counsel from the wise, nor the word from the prophet" (Jer. 18:18). We find these all—all these styles—in Christ. We are reminded of the lines from Shakespeare's sonnet:

> What is thy substance, whereof art thou made,
> That thousands of strange shadows on thee tend!

We can pursue this further. Nearest of kin to the parables of Jesus are those of the Jewish rabbis. But the parable, or *mashal,* as they used it was rooted in the wisdom tradition of Israel,[9] associated with Solomon, but going far back beyond him in the ancient love of clever speech and trope among the Hebrews, and especially the Egyptians. It is a moving thought

---

9. The *mashal* is a dominant feature of the biblical wisdom literature. In this literature, it is true, we have mainly single tropes, expanded proverbs, and metaphorical aphorisms, rather than developed stories. But the Old Testament and ancient tradition of the East provide ample evidence of the story-parable.

that the incomparable and destiny-fraught parables of Jesus are directly linked with generations and millenniums of human delight in the apt word and the felicitous image.

Now if the parables of Jesus came out of the wisdom tradition to Israel, we also know today that apocalyptic was closely related to wisdom. If Solomon was seen as the founder of proverbial wisdom, Enoch, for example, was a chief representative of wisdom of another kind.[10] Jesus' eschatological outlook and imagery were related to the latter, as his parables were to the former. He united both styles and brought both into direct relation with the realities of his time.

Indeed, there are parables in the apocalyptic literature of Judaism and in its intertestamental writings which illuminate Jesus' use of this form. In the Book of Enoch, the term *mashal* is prominent in the sense of a "revelation of the secrets of God concerning the economy of salvation, relative to the person and work of the Messiah as well as to the destiny of the good and the evil."[11] Thus in Enoch (as in the oracles of Balaam in Numbers, chaps. 23–24) a parable or *mashal* means a prophetic unveiling of the secrets of the future. In intertestamental Judaism there was a tendency for the older categories to be merged—law and wisdom, but also wisdom and prophecy or apocalyptic vision.[12]

It is true that Jesus' parables of the Kingdom are not strictly unveilings of the secrets of the heavenly realm in the sense of its geography or its angelic and demonic orders. But they have the character of prophetic revelation,[13] as is not the case with the rabbinic parables, or most of them. On the other hand, they are like the latter in that they are firmly planted in human life. The parables of Jesus thus draw upon both the wisdom mode of the rabbis and that of the seers. But in this connection also we must say that a greater than Jonah is here, and a greater than Solomon.

The rhetorical perfection of the parables of Jesus could lead a reader

10. See Pierre Grelot, "La Légende d'Henoch dans les Apocryphes et dans la Bible," *Recherches de science réligieuse* 46:5–26, 181–210.

11. Hermaniuk, *La Parabole*, p. 130.

12. See R. E. Brown, "The Pre-Christian Semitic Concept of 'Mystery,' " *Catholic Biblical Quarterly* 20 (1958), pp. 417–43; and "The Semitic Background of the New Testament *mysterion*, 1–2," *Biblica* 39 (1958), pp. 426–48; 40 (1959), pp. 70–87. (These essays have been reprinted as *The Semitic Background of the Term "Mystery" in the New Testament* in Facet Books [Philadelphia: Fortress Press, 1968].)

13. At this point, and elsewhere in this chapter, I am indebted to the discussions in the graduate New Testament Seminar at the Harvard Divinity School, which dealt with the topic of the Gospel parables in the fall semester of 1961–62, under the chairmanship of Prof. Krister Stendahl.

to think of him as essentially a teacher, and as a rather dispassionate one at that, an artist. We do not easily reconcile such fastidious concern with form with eschatological fervor and passion. Prophetic inspiration, we think, must necessarily give us outbursts of passion, rather than the kind of classic rhetoric of these parables. Some are tempted, therefore, to say that the Jesus of the parables alone is the real Jesus, and that the fanciful and perfervid sayings of an apocalyptic kind cannot be authentic. The Jesus of the parables is sane; the Jesus who speaks of the Son of man coming with the clouds is fanatical. The Jesus of the parables is a true humanist; the eschatological Jesus is a cloudy visionary.

In such judgments we are misled by modern categories of classic and romantic. We associate artistic forms of speech like those of the parables with cool and polished workmanship, repeatedly worked over and brought to perfection. We associate what seem eloquent outbursts of vision with unpremeditated inspiration and even ecstasy. Our own predisposition may lead us to prefer one to the other. With respect to Jesus, in any case, we are puzzled. We have, on the one hand, the parables, and such patterned and strophic sayings as those evoking the lilies of the field and the fowl of the air. And we have, on the other hand, such sayings as "I beheld Satan as lightning fallen from heaven. Behold, I give unto you power to tread on serpents and scorpions and over all the powers of the enemy: and nothing shall by any means hurt you" (Luke 10:18–19) (KJV); or "Then shall they see the Son of man coming in the clouds with great power and glory. And then shall he send his angels, and shall gather together his elect from the four winds, from the uttermost part of the earth to the uttermost part of heaven" (Mark 13:26–27) (KJV).

But what we should recognize, as Ernst Käsemann has said, is that felicity and sophistication of form are perfectly compatible with prophetic and, indeed, extempore utterance.[14] Thus the parable of the sower, for instance, can well be seen as prophetic, rather than sapiential. The aesthetic balance of Jesus' sayings about serving two masters or about the straight gate and the broad way, similarly, can represent prophetic improvisation. In any case, they have the immediate impulse that goes with their oral character. The point is that Jesus transcends all these dichotomies. The same issue arises with respect to the hymns and oracles produced by the church after the resurrection, powerful and concentrated rhetorical utterances which we find cited both in the epistles and in the Gospels. These

---

14. "Die Anfänge christlicher Theologie," *ZTK* 57 (1960):174, and see there n. 2. (Reprinted as "The Beginnings of Christian Theology" in *New Testament Questions of Today*, tr. W. J. Montague [Philadelphia: Fortress Press, 1969], pp. 82–107.)

have poetic form. For example, we can cite the jubilant formulas found in chapters two and three of the Apocalypse, of which one instance is:

> To him that overcometh will I grant to
> sit with me in my throne,
> even as I also overcame, and am set
> down with my Father in his throne (3:21) (KJV).

Or we can cite as such an oracle the words found on the lips of Jesus:

> Whoever says a word against the Son of man will be forgiven; but whoever speaks against the Holy Spirit will not be forgiven, either in this age or in the age to come (Matt. 12:32) (KJV).

Now Käsemann rightly says, with regard to such early Christian apocalyptic testimonies, "Primitive Christianity as is shown both in its hymns and in the 'He who overcomes' sayings in Revelation, did in fact ascribe to the Spirit this precise capacity of combining concentrated content and artistic form."[15]

Returning to the parables of Jesus, we conclude that their artistic form does not make them in any way incompatible with Jesus' eschatological sayings. Nor should we think of them as artistically premeditated, in contrast with other sayings seen as ejaculations or outbursts. Even in the case of the parables, we are confronted with that immediacy and presence of the speaker which we have stressed in connection with the oral features of all Jesus' communication.

III. THE PARABLES AND THE KINGDOM

Let us select for attention those parables which are usually spoken of as the parables of the Kingdom. We find these in the fourth chapter of Mark —the parables of the sower, the seed growing of itself, and the mustard seed. And we select from the thirteenth chapter of Matthew also those of the leaven, the hidden treasure, and the pearl of great price. We extricate these parables from the contexts in which the evangelists place them, and we try to identify their original form by taking account of any parallels and of recastings. We also disregard, for the time being, the interpretations assigned there to Jesus of the parable of the sower.

Now we have good reason to believe that we have reached bedrock with

---

15. Ibid., p. 96. Further, with reference to the sayings of Jesus about Jonah and the Queen of the South, Matt. 12.41ff., Käsemann writes, "Only a false conception of inspiration as resulting in an uncontrolled outburst of feeling can enter this [such poetic form] in evidence against the presence of prophecy here" (*New Testament Questions*, p. 95).

this material. There is wide agreement that it is in the parables that we can feel confidence that we hear Jesus of Nazareth speaking. We have a natural desire to identify precisely his authentic words, the *ipsissima verba*. The importance of this should not be overestimated. We can know Jesus historically through the eyes and through the hearts of his immediate followers, even if they do not remember his words exactly, and even when they quite understandably adapt, supplement, and generalize them, not to speak of those which they forget or pass over. Even when they put words in his mouth, these, too, may convey to us the reality of the founder in what is most essential. Jesus' creative speech was so fresh and significant that it could, as it were, breed speech true to itself. We have an analogy of this phenomenon when we say that certain stories about Abraham Lincoln may not be authentic, but they are true to Lincoln.

Yet we naturally seek to identify the actual words of Jesus. One of the criteria for this is form, and here, evidently, the parable offers a very tangible example. The characteristic design, the tight form, of these utterances helped to guarantee them against change and supplementation. A coherent image-story is resistant to change. One can press putty into different shapes, but not a crystal. A crystal can pick up foreign material, but we can recognize the difference. Here especially if a thing is well said, there is only one way to say it, as in a poem. These parables of Jesus have an organic unity and coherence. They come down through retelling protected by their shape and hardness like quartz nuggets in a stream. This organic unity, say of the parable of the seed growing of itself, or of the sower, derives from the fact that each one represents an imaginative vision. All the aspects fall into place. Each one is a little drama seen as a whole.

One can raise the question whether followers of Jesus could not have created one or other of these parables. We do not need to be jealous for Jesus in this respect. We should be ready to admit that a sonnet ascribed to Shakespeare or a painting ascribed to Rembrandt is not, as we say, genuine. But there are criteria. Such criteria have always something of the subjective about them. As a matter of fact, there is some reason to think that the parable of the tares is not genuine. Such tests are verisimilitude, force, relevance, dependence on other parables, and, in the case of the parable of the tares, all of these considerations converge to arouse our suspicions.

The acid tests for Jesus' parables are what I would call focus and depth. There is no blurring in them, or incongruity. Moreover, they are not discursive. All this springs from the depth of concern and intensity of vision. It is not fair, perhaps, to contrast Paul here, since he is discoursing in another vein. But it is well known that his metaphors drawn from building operations or agriculture reflect a different kind of inspiration. There are elements of incongruity in them arising from an allegorical procedure, just as there are in some of Jesus' parables in those aspects which reflect later supplementation by his followers.

Let us return to this matter of the criteria for the authenticity of Jesus' sayings. We find our confidence at the maximum in his parables. I would go further, and say in certain kinds of his parables, especially these parables of the Kingdom. Some of his parables, such as these, are in their nature more closely knit, more clearly shaped by a single vision. They are therefore less subject to modification. They can be interpreted like the parable of the sower, but they cannot easily be revised; and if they are revised, the revision betrays itself. But Jesus' illustrative stories have great variety. He used images with sovereign freedom and in very different veins. Therefore there are some of what we call his parables which are indeed distinctive and powerful, but looser in texture, not requiring the same inevitability and design. And there are some whose flexible variation in the telling is already clearly evident in the Gospels, as well as in the later church, such parables as those of the watchful servants, the feast, the pounds or talents. Such parables may often have been occasioned by particular pedagogical or controversial occasions. Their mintage was therefore different. They lent themselves to new applications. It is more difficult to recover the original wording.

Another formal consideration bearing on the authenticity of Jesus' parables takes us farther afield. It is the role of image and metaphor in his speech generally. In the parables, we have action images. But these are only one kind of metaphor—extended metaphor. Jesus' communication, just because it is fresh and dynamic, is necessarily plastic. Now we know that a true metaphor or symbol is more than a sign, it is a bearer of the reality to which it refers. The hearer not only learns about that reality, he participates in it. He is invaded by it. Here lie the power and fatefulness of art. Jesus' speech had the character, not of instruction and ideas, but of compelling imagination, of spell, of mythical shock and transformation. Not just in an aesthetic sense, but in the service of the Gospel. Now, just as Jesus used trope and metaphor in the most varied way, so with his narrative images. But in either case, we have a criterion for his authentic words in the force and significance of the imagery.

With this question of the significance of the imagery, we can return to the parables of the Kingdom. Let us have in mind first Mark's parables of the sower, of the seed growing of itself, and of the mustard seed. We have seen that with respect to form and texture they fall into the type of action images; their minting represents a single act of total vision; they are prophetic in character, rather than discursive or argumentative.

Now, is it enough to say that in the parable of the sower, for example, Jesus offers encouragement to his disciples over against the inevitable setbacks and disappointments of the preaching of the Kingdom; the farmer loses some seed here, some seed there, but in the outcome there is abundant—even superabundant—harvest? If we read the parable somewhat prosaically, this is where we come out. And this kind of reading soon passes over into various applications and point-for-point allegory, all of which may be instructive, but are lacking in any momentous significance. This would have meant, then, that Jesus led his disciples and ourselves to trust in God's overruling of difficulties. But this parable is surely not just an example of what happens every day, offered as an encouragement. That would be banal. The hearer could say, "Well, sometimes the farmers are rewarded this way, sometimes not." Thus this kind of interpretation, I repeat, really offers only a kind of commonplace. Taken in this way, the parable itself falls down. As Ernst Fuchs has observed, a farmer hopes that he will have a large crop; he usually does; but there is nothing in the nature of the case that guarantees it; drought or other calamity may ruin the year's operation. Therefore the illustration in itself offers no cogent assurance to the faith of the disciple. At the best, in these terms, the parable says what we can hear on all sides from men of courage and hopefulness.

Similarly with the parable of the seed growing of itself, and we confine ourselves to the verses Mark 4:26–28:

> And he said, "The Kingdom of God is as if a man should scatter seed upon the ground, and should sleep and rise night and day, and the seed should sprout and grow, he knows not how. The earth produces of itself, first the blade, then the ear, then the full grain in the ear."

Again, we take this too often in a banal sense. Jesus' disciples learned that they could trust the secret working of God. In the parable of the mustard seed, we have the same confidence inspired, though here the emphasis falls on the disproportion between the small beginnings and the great outcomes. But this again can be banal; we have heard it before.

Fortunately, we usually see more in these parables than this, because we come at them in the context of the Christian faith, the Christian mystery. But we must go all the way in this matter of context, and see them in Jesus' own situation. Then their real authority and power emerge. It is Jesus' own certain faith that paints in the feature of the great harvest. The formal felicity and coherence of these parables reflect the intensity of his own vision. The parable of the sower is a prophetic, and not a discursive parable, a metaphor of faith. The realism, however, testifies to the fact that that faith and expectation are identified with daily life and with God's operation there. The disciples are heartened, not by a homiletic illustration drawn from nature, but by Jesus' impartation to them of his own vision, by the power of metaphor. For us, too, to find the meaning of the parable we must identify ourselves with that inner secret of Jesus' faith and faithfulness. To quote again from Fuchs: "The distinctive feature in the teaching aspects of Jesus' proclamation is the analogical power with which tacitly he sets forth himself, his own obedience, as a measure for the attention of his disciples."[16]

Objection may be raised to this understanding of the parables which links their significance with Jesus himself. There has been too much of a dogmatic view according to which the figure and authority of Christ is read into and forced upon the parables. Thus the sower in these parables is identified with Christ. But he is also, in other parables, identified as the pearl of great price, or even as the thief who breaks in when not expected, and so forth. We, for our part, are not insisting on a Christological interpretation of the parables in any such sense. But we are saying that they should be understood in relation to the speaker and the occasion; not in connection with his titles, but in relation to his way and his goal.

If we bring in the twin parables of the treasure in the field and the pearl of great price, we can enlarge our discussion. Let us quote the former:

> The kingdom of heaven is like treasure hidden in a field, which a man found and covered up; then in his joy he goes and sells all that he has and buys the field (Matt. 13:44).

As Joachim Jeremias says, the emphasis here is not on the value of the treasure nor on the sacrifice involved, but on the joy in the discovery. This joy feature is implicit in the seed parables, with their sense of marvel and expectation, just as it comes to expression in the beatitudes, which are to be understood as congratulatory, rather than hortatory.

The historical Jesus comes into better focus if we see him as using two media to proclaim the Kingdom—in addition to his action, of course. On the one hand, he used eschatological imagery and categories. "The Kingdom of God is at hand." He spoke of the judgment, the Messianic banquet, the

16. *Hermeneutik*, 2nd ed. (Bad Cannstatt: R. Müllerschön Verlag, 1958), p. 228. This statement and its elaboration by Fuchs locate one focus of the contemporary discussion of the parables, especially in connection with the new quest of the historical Jesus. Cf. Fuchs, *Hermeneutik*, sec. 17, and "Bemerkungen zur Gleichnisauslegung," in his *Zur Frage nach dem historischen Jesus* (Tübingen: J. C. B. Mohr [Paul Siebeck], 1960), pp. 136–42.

life of the age to come, perhaps of the heavenly Son of man coming with the clouds of heaven. All this was the available theological symbol of his time and place. But he said the same things in what we can call layman's language in his parables of the Kingdom, parables of judgment, and so forth. What does this mean except that he brought theology down into daily life and into the immediate everyday situation? Here is a clue for the modern preacher, indeed for the Christian whatever his form of witness.

In both his eschatological and his parable announcement, we have the note of joy. Behind both again is the sense of the power and grace of God at work and the wonder and promise of the outcome. Jesus testifies to all this confidence in his parables, but also to the requisite decision and devotion and, indeed, to the endurance and suffering involved. The parables we have been concerned with all involve an action, a narrative—associated with life as it is—and the features of waiting, endurance, and striving are variously included. The full significance of all this is only lifted above the banal and commonplace if we recognize the momentousness of that to which Jesus himself witnesses. His eschatological language is one indication of it. The parables, even including their form, are another. The church later identified this momentousness of the parables by finding in them the "mystery" of the Kingdom of God.

I myself choose a trope or parable to suggest this significance of the Gospel and of the rhetoric of faith employed by Jesus. The French poet St. John Perse, in his address on the occasion of receiving the Nobel Prize for literature, spoke of the power of language, especially of the power of the image-maker the poet. He had the audacity to compare that power with that of nuclear energy. He did not hesitate to set the fragile clay lamp of the poet over against the atomic oven as source of world-transformation. Unimagined futures lie folded as in a seed in a new creative word, in the birth of language in an emerging myth.

This is a dim analogy of the power of the Gospel and of the dawning Kingdom of God as Jesus knew it and brought it to expression in his parables as well as in his eschatological sayings. It is this kind of authority, certainly, that voices itself in the seed parables—aware of cost and ordeal, but also of joy. If the poet's clay lamp is ultimately more determinative than the atomic oven, we hear in the Gospel also of a lamp set on a stand where it gives light to all in the house; and of a city which "has no need of sun or moon to shine upon it, for the glory of God is its light, and its lamp is the Lamb" (Rev. 21:23).

The parables, finally, permit us to make one observation about the founder of Christianity which transcends our discussion hitherto. In these sayings we have the one element in the Gospels of any extent which, after due sifting, we can hold as original with little question. What do these sayings tell us about Jesus? They tell us that we have here a Jewish mind and heart at that precise point of the heritage where the particular religious tradition becomes indistinguishable from universal humanity, where religion becomes secular without loss, where Israel becomes Adam, the law becomes the way of mankind, and the son of Abraham becomes the Son of man. The humanity and secularity of Jesus, it should be emphasized, is not, however, to be confused with humanist, romantic, or aesthetic ideals, though it includes all that these quests seek. In the Jesus of the parables we have a humanity in which, uniquely, the heart of man is recognized as is not the case in all such humanisms, and yet in a way which is universal.

3

Telling From
Depth to Depth:
The Parable of the Sower

I. DEEP REGISTERS OF RESPONSE

It is now widely evident that an important new phase of New Testament study is emerging. The initiatives are various, but they all have to do with a deeper inquiry into the nature of language and "how language works." The focus is well suggested by the title of a recent book by Paul Ricoeur dealing mainly with biblical texts: *The Theological Bearings of Contemporary Investigations with Respect to Language.*[1]

The basic concern remains that of *meaning* and of language as communication. Therefore the various thrusts all come under the wider caption of hermeneutics. But it is increasingly felt that the dynamics and import of discourse, the full meaning of a biblical passage, go beyond what our usual methods of exegesis and interpretation convey. Words and phrases, narrations and liturgical poems or other speech modes, require other resources for their understanding than those provided by our usual philological, historical, and theological expertise. There are certain resonances and imponderables in language, whether in folktales or in the highest literary art, which are often felt by the layman, but their operations should be brought to light and understood if we are to have any full interpretation of a writing.

A work of art has a life of its own apart from its reporters. It remains itself and goes on testifying or celebrating, independently of its interpreters and their various versions and deformations of its communication.[2] So it

1. Paul Ricoeur, *Les Incidences théologiques des recherches actuelles concernant le langage* (Paris: Institut d'Etudes Oecumeniques, n.d.).

2. Paul Ricoeur, "Le symbole n'a jamais fini de donner à dire." *Le Conflit des interprétations* (Paris: du Seuil, 1969), p. 32.

is with a parable or other literary form in Scripture. Its *telling* is ever and again to be heard naively and afresh. The deep registers of response in the hearer should not be disturbed at this level of encounter by other pre-occupations.

But then comes the phase of wider understanding, of relating this communication to others and to our whole context of meaning and reality. Since the mystery and operations of language are involved, we find ourselves committed to clarification at this point, so that we can give a better account of our "hearing" and the terms of its interpretation. With respect to a parable, this means an understanding of its language structure, its poetic. But it also means an understanding of how this language dynamically evokes response, its semantic.

II. EPIPHANIC DISCLOSURES

If I may be allowed a personal reminiscence, I adduce the following experience. In a rural Sunday school class taught by a village housewife in ways surely contrary to all the precepts of the religious educator, the parable of the sower was the theme, no doubt assigned in some long-since-repudiated graded lesson book. I was fourteen at the time, and my reaction may have been colored by the fact that I was working on a farm that summer. In any case, I have always recalled with wonder the impact, the imaginative reverberations, and the psychic dynamics of the six verses of the parable. (I am sure that the allegorizing interpretation of the parable that follows it in the Gospel did not disturb this prior visionary transaction.) This revelatory power of the parable was no doubt related to the fresh sensibility of childhood, but the experience has always remained with me as one of my earliest memories of the power of Scripture and of language generally. Over and above all rules and resources of interpretation later acquired, I had learned in this instance to respect the naked text itself, to let the word and the words have their own untrammeled course, to be open to their deeper signals, to let the naïf speak to the naïf and depth to depth.

But one need not leave it there, or at this level. We rightly seek to understand the operations of the imagination and the heart. This is, first of all, a native and proper impulse of our human nature to organize our experience and to relate reason to the prerational. Even the deepest layers of sensibility have their laws and structures. To trace them out and to become aware of them is to enter more fully into possession of our being. It is also to illuminate the processes of new creativity and vision, and to further them. One could illustrate by the art of music and the interplay here of the composer's command of its "laws" and structures with his ultimate impulse. But our concern is with the arts of language.

If one were to exemplify this double approach, the naive and the structural, in the case of the parable of the sower we might illuminate the wider issue. What lighted up my imagination as a boy exposed to an emblematic story was the nevertheless prevailing power of the sown seed, indeed its extravagant yield, but also the deep wedding of the venture of the sower with this prevailing. It was not first of all a question of the sower nor of the vicissitudes of his operation, nor was it a question of the various soils. But all these in combination provided the analogue for the inexorable and indefeasible continuity and plenitude of creation of which man is a part.

Accepting some such reading or hearing of the parable as an unsophisticated depth-response, what can one say about it as a language vehicle? What is the correlation of form and communication? What observations about its rhetoric or linguistic structure would help to explain its power and to disentangle its real focus? Inadequate interpretations of the parable are certainly connected with inattention to its literary features. If it is not read as a distinctive form or artistic whole, alien motifs from a wider context in the gospel or the chapter are introduced. So one is carried into illegitimate allegorization (from the sequel, Mark 4:13ff.), or into the search for some esoteric teaching (Mark 4:11–12), or for direct light on the teacher and his work. If the parable is not grasped as (extended) metaphor, the reader will then look for a teaching or a theme, rather than a revelatory shock of insight.

That shock of insight is related both to the aesthetic form of the utterance and to the receptivity of the hearer. Therefore we speak both of the "poetic" and the "semantic" of the New Testament texts. The two are related. A parable or a saying or a prayer have a given form because they have long been shaped in that way among those concerned, who are therefore ready to hear something in such and such a pattern. The medium already locates the communication. If the pattern and style are associated with visionary insight, rather than with instruction or mandate, then the hearer attends to it in this mode and expectation. The tone of voice of the speaker would further this reception. (It is only when our parable was in written form that it would invite the kind of piecemeal scrutiny that led to allegory and be read as paraenesis.)

III. BETWEEN ANGUISH AND TRUST

The simplest way to explore the dynamics of our parable is to ask what there is about it as "words" that would make it interesting to the hearer or hold his attention. (We can leave out here the identity of the speaker.) First, it is a story; it is narrative with the world-old appeal of "What happened?" "What happened next?" "How did it turn out?" Second, it is a kind of riddle or teaser, with the similar appeal of "what does it mean?" "What is he getting at?" Third, it is a conventional or artistic form, which arouses expectation of special import, as well as delight in felicitous speech. Fourth, it evokes familiar matters in wholly appropriate locutions and persuasiveness. An initiated audience delights in exact mimetic detail, in cogent actuality, just as its attention is forfeited by any lack of verisimilitude in this kind of narrative. Fifth, the aesthetic medium or genre form lifts the diurnal level of the action into another context, with new overtones. (A metaphor is a "transaction between contexts"—I.A. Richards— which, therefore, by the tension created, excites a deeper attention.) An aesthetic form dynamizes its raw material, whether ordinary perception or generalized feeling, converting them into vision, thus acting as a kind of prism. (Contrast the tenor of the parable of the sower with the case where a peasant would merely report the equivalent sequence of his operations to a neighbor as a passing topic of conversation.)

But there are other, and deeper, levels in the language of the parable which need to be accounted for in dealing with its power of communication. There are correspondences between its rhetorical features and human response beyond those cited. Here is where we meet the contemporary discussion of structures with respect to language and literature.

Nearer the surface in biblical anecdotes and fictions, we find features common to storytelling anywhere in the world ("laws of epic style," etc.). As in folktales and children's stories, we find brevity, unity of perspective, limitation of the number of figures or agents, use of direct discourse, serial development, the "rule of three," repetition of elements and formulas, binary opposition, and resolution often by reversal. Or our analysis may cut another way, and proceed in terms of recurrent plot-patterns, or topoi, or motifs. Human nature has always responded to stories about quests and adventures, ups and downs, rags to riches, lost and found, reversals and surprises; stories about tricksters and strategems; about duels and conflicts —between the good and bad son or daughter, perhaps; of Greek meeting Greek; stories of magical transformations and wonders. Biblical narratives rejoin universal storytelling in their repertoire of motifs; masters and servants, the wise and the foolish, rewards and penalties, success and failure.

In the parable of the sower, our response and expectation are quickened by the five features mentioned at the beginning of this section. We also note the "rule of three," thrice instanced: three types of loss; three verbs of bringing forth ("growing up," "increasing," "yielding"); three degrees of increment (thirtyfold, sixtyfold, one hundredfold). We also observe the feature of reversal and surprise, the fourth case against the first three. But this denouement or resolution is also marked by (at least rhetorical) hyperbole.

There is, indeed, a question as to whether the yield—thirtyfold, sixty-fold, one hundredfold—represents an extraordinary outcome. (It refers not to the whole sowing, but to the seed sown on the good soil.) Here Linnemann rejects Jeremias's view to that effect as a misunderstanding of Dalman's data. But apart from this uncertainty, two considerations argue for taking the yield as hyperbolic and a departure from realism: 1) The ascending serial enumeration, in the context of the art form, intensifies the feature of surprise and disproportion. The imagination is pointed even beyond the hundredfold. Thus at least rhetorical hyperbole. 2) The motif of disproportion is paralleled in other parables like that of the leaven, and in another parable of growth, that of the mustard seed.[3]

These various features of the parable, shared with universal patterns of fabulation, identify it with an imaginative genre or art convention which, as I have said, dynamizes its "raw material." The medium alerts the hearer to a wider horizon of import. That a genre medium is in question is also indicated by the initial ἰδοῦ (Listen!), as it would have been in any case in the oral telling by a subtle change in the tone of voice and delivery.

If one presses this matter of our responses to particular rhetorical features or signals in a story or a text, one comes to something still more fundamental. There is indeed something in us that answers to the kinds of patterns of speech and motifs suggested. But among these are some that go very deep into our emotion and imagination and motivation. We can think of the self as containing, as it were, explosive material, which can only be kindled by the appropriate art or language. Psychology can speak of archetypes. The study of dreams, mythology, and folklore can uncover recurrent structures of consciousness, scenarios of wish, anxiety, and fulfillment. When we speak of the appeal of a poem to the imagination, this

---

3. The seeming exception of another "parable of growth," the parable of the "seed growing of itself" that yields finally only "the full grain in the ear," has a different movement and a different horizon, that of the time when the sower returns to "put in the sickle." In any case, in this parable, the aspect of miraculous operation is associated with the αὐτομάτη of the fruit-bearing. The Greek term does not mean "of itself," but "without any recognizable cause," or "by the operation of God." See R. Stuhlmann, "Beobachtungen und Überlegungen zu Markus 4:26–29," *New Testament Studies* 19 (1972–73):153–62. Stuhlmann, like Jeremias, includes v. 29 in the original parable.

is part of what we mean, especially in connection with the power of symbols. But even apart from powerful inherited social imagery, there are kinds of language which engage these deep structures.

Jesus could use such dynamic images as Kingdom or Satan or Gehenna. But he could also use plot patterns (such as lost and found) or role situations (master and servant) which similarly engage our deepest apperceptions. The master-servant relation evokes the archetype of authority deeply buried in the human psyche, an archetype which is ambivalent and charged with both anxiety and the craving for security. In the case of the parable of the sower, I see two deep sounding boards that lend power to the communication and enter into its proper interpretation. These are like inflammable tinder awaiting its fuse: charged language.

For one thing, man's relation to the earth and its processes is primordial and full of mystery. Folklore, mythology, and the "savage mind" see tilling and planting as transactions with powers, chthonic and divine, and harvest as having the character of miracle. Our parable, as an art form, identifies itself with this naive depth. In contrast, perhaps, with the parable of the mustard seed, this one (and that of the seed growing $αὐτομάτη$) involves the husbandman. It has to do with culture, and not with wild nature alone. The enigmatic vicissitudes of loss and gain involve man's place in creation and its exuberance, the primordial wonder that existence emerges out of, and prevails over, nothingness. If one speaks of "structure" here, it would refer to an internalized pattern in the psyche which dictates such universal motifs as those of the garden, Paradise, and other archetypes, in dreams and human fabulation.

A second sounding board evoked in the parable goes even deeper. It relates to man's ultimate *conatas,* or striving, or going out from himself in search of fulfillment. Our very being and security in existence are strangely poised between trust and lack of trust. Man is a conative, intentional project, and there is profound existential drama at the core of his nature between the sense of being sustained in his venture and anguish at betrayal. The parable speaks out of, and to, this dynamic turmoil by assurance not only of the trustworthiness of existence, but of its plenitude and excess.

Our parable speaks to this particular sounding board or register in the hearer in terms of sower, seed, soils, and harvest. What is here presented in the language-analogue of the husbandman or the archetype of the garden could equally well be dramatized or storied in some other metaphor of human activity. The basic paradigm of man's initiative vis-à-vis his world and its sequel could employ other types of venture: not only sowing, but fishing, and also hunting, digging, mining; risking, investing, gambling. The Gospels include some of these motifs or fields of action in various rhetorical forms to reveal one or other face of the vision conveyed in the parable of the sower. We think, for example, of the parable of the friend at midnight. However, the basic paradigm of effort and reward can take a brief, imperative form: "Ask, and it will be given you; seek, and you will find; knock, and it will be opened to you." The paradigm of effort and reward would then be seen as the *structural* formula (open to various versions of "generative poetic"), the formula itself, however, resting for its power on an ontological depth.

It is, then, not only in the parable genre that this particular sounding board finds dramatization in the Gospel. In the "legend" (as it is called by Bultmann and Dibelius) of the miraculous draught of fishes in Luke 5:4–10 (also reported in John 21), we find the same scenario and elements as in the parable of the sower, but here in the context of fishing, rather than planting. By "scenario," I mean the sequence of 1) initiative vis-à-vis nature, 2) frustration, and 3) extravagant outcome. The dynamics of the narrative again arise out of a deep human constant: man poised between trust and anguish in his relation to existence: "Master, we toiled all night and took nothing!" The dynamics of the narrative also arise, at a second level, from the employment here of a folklore motif,[4] or more generally from the sea-wonder category of the narrative. Corresponding to the "thirtyfold, sixtyfold, one hundredfold" of the parable of the sower, we have in the legend, "And when they had done this, they enclosed a great shoal of fish. . . . Their nets were breaking. . . . They filled both the boats, so that they began to sink." The correspondence of the scenarios in the two genres points to a common underlying vision of reality.[5] But we have been interested in the patterns of language by which this vision is mediated.

Returning to the parable of the sower, we may well ask why its culminating reassurance has cogency. The analogy of the yield of the good soil is not persuasive in itself. Romantic consolations drawn from aspects of nature are notoriously subjective. The very language of such "effusions"

4. E. Klostermann's view, questioned by Rudolph Bultmann, *The History of the Synoptic Tradition,* tr. John Marsh, (New York: Harper & Row, 1973), p. 217. Indirectly relevant is the vision in Ezek. 47:9–10 of the eschatological abundance of fish in the life-giving water of the great river issuing from the threshold of the temple, of the "spreading of nets" and of "the very many kinds of fish, like the fish of the Great Sea."

5. It is of more than incidental interest that Luke introduces the legend in a setting (Jesus teaching from the boat) and with phrases which in Mark lead to the parable of the sower.

betrays their inconsequence. Their rhetoric lays hold of no subsoil deeper than sentiment or euphoria; simile and allegory take the place of metaphor; apostrophe and exclamation points are poor surrogates for vision.

The success story told in our parable is not bland propaganda for optimism. There is too much economy, tension, and aesthetic distance in the language.[6] As with a poem, the parable form as a distinctive kind of voice, and by its architecture, reveals rather than persuades. So far as it persuades, it is not by an induction, but by a visionary recognition. This recognition has to do, not with optimistic eudaemonism, but with the creaturely sense of the trustworthiness of existence. If this sense is threatened by panic or anguish, the parable lights up the inner theater of travail and speaks reassurance—recalling us to a prior vision of reality—as Jesus did to Peter when Peter's faith failed and he began to sink in the sea.

IV. PARABLE AND PARABLER

In exploring the language of the parable, I have called attention to certain rhetorical features and to two sounding boards or structures to which it appeals. These considerations help us to understand its impact at any time or place. But then we have the question as to the speaker, and therewith that of his situation and audience. Here it would seem that we step outside the rhetorical form itself. Yet since we have to do with language and communication, even so self-ordered a trope as a parable witnesses to its author *in its own way,* and to the situation of its utterance.

His authority in the original occasion can be dissociated from that assumed for him in the Gospel context in which we now find the parable. We can also set aside interpretations of the parable of the sower according to which Jesus would have transparently referred to himself in the role of the sower. But then we encounter the persuasive view that the faith of Jesus himself in and through the travail of his calling is meditated by his disciples through this compelling and revelatory metaphor. Thus the parable interprets Jesus' action in the situation, while at the same time being sanctioned by him as the speaker.

---

6. The confining rules and formal aspects of a poem or other genre, these exacting features of its "poetic," serve as barriers to false lyricism. This has been brought out recently in connection with W. H. Auden, who, to avoid "easy Eloquence," finds a need of "complex resistances [metrics]" and of "inhibitors: syntactical, grammatical, lexical." In his *Epistle to a Godson and Other Poems* (New York: Random House, 1972, p. 47) Auden puts it this way:

> Blessed be all metrical rules that
> forbid automatic responses,
> force us to have second thoughts,
> free from the fetters of Self.

In the original oral situation, Jesus does not impose consent by extrinsic authority. It is indirectly, in the fictional world of the saying, that his role as Master and Teacher operates. In his address and solicitation to the hearers (made explicit in the later written form by the introduction "Listen!" and by the concluding words "He that has ears to hear, let him hear"), he does indeed relate the action of the parable to the public occasion, and therefore to his own work and mission. But consent to his cause and person goes *pari passu* with consent to the affirmation of the parable itself. Here is where we find the "through-meaning" (Via) of the dense and self-sufficient fiction. And in any later context down to our own, there is some such interplay between the parable and the "authority" under which it is presented (Jesus as the Christ, the Church, the Scripture, a given preacher or teacher, or some combination of these). But in all such changing contexts, the parable continues to have a life of its own, and one that continually challenges and corrects current deformations of its deeper import.

With respect to the "audience" or hearers, there are many variables. Jesus' immediate hearers were at home with the parable genre, if in a somewhat different rabbinic form. Absence of familiarity with this particular shape of narrative handicaps its right reception, as is already evident in the New Testament. Even the basic psychological structures to which the parable speaks can vary. While men of all cultures would share to some extent in the two "sounding boards" I have cited, there would be differences. Man's sense of his relation to nature varies in different cultural settings, given all the uniformities of sowing and reaping. More significantly, the basic correspondence posited and confirmed in the parable between human striving and fulfillment could be assumed in the Hebraic context. But there have been, and are, great cultural areas and epochs in which the *conatus* is anemic, and in which willing, intention, action are not deeply related to the reality-sense. It would be interesting to see how motifs of sowing, fishing, and hunting are manipulated in non-Western fabulation. In gnostic versions of the biblical stories, one can recognize a transformation.

V. MISCARRIAGE AND FRUITION

I have said that the parable proffers a vision of the selective vivacity or exuberance of life over against its wide miscarriage. At the core of the vision and at the heart of the parable is the motif of miscarriage or waste. This note three times invoked is not only a foil to the extravagant outcome, as it might be in a romantic analogue; it is part of the mystery of the total transaction, a transaction which has its dead ends and blind alleys. God finds his way through miscarriage and impasse to incommensurable fruition. But of course in the generality of the metaphor, there is no identification of the losses.

It is this aspect of selectivity to which attention is drawn in the allegorizing interpretation of the parable given in Mark 4:14-20, with a paraenetic intention and with an individualizing application. The same is true of the section Mark 4:10-13, with its distinction between "those outside" and those who receive the secret of the Kingdom of God. In this focus on the mystery of rejection, these later supplements relate to the depth of the parable.

The double motif of selection and fruition cannot but remind us of Israel's understanding of calling and rejection—"Jacob I loved, but Esau I hated"—and the theme of the remnant. The world-story has its dead ends and discards, both within and without the line of election, but it goes on, and the lavish future lies with the elect, more in number than the sands of the sea. The parable is too autonomous a creation to be allegorized in this sense. But the deep paradigm resonates in it and conditions the "answering imagination" of the hearers.[7]

Even deeper than this appeal to Israel's own apperception, the language and "plot" of the parable relate it, as we have seen, to elementary human striving, frustration, and fulfillment. Through the theme of miscarriage, we can hear such laments as that of Jeremiah 51:58:

> The peoples labor for nought,
> and the nations weary themselves only for fire.

The parable brings both these levels into relation to Jesus' ministry and proclamation in such a way as to empower consent.

In this light, it is not necessary to declare an impasse, as Linnemann does, with respect to the occasion and meaning of the parable—even to the point of envisaging its nonauthenticity. It is true that there is no particular

---

7. This same profound paradigm is, of course, prominent, and as a problem, in 2 Esdras. Note 8:41, a passage in which the husbandman's sowing illustrates the larger theme of the remnant and "the multitude of those who perish." "For just as the farmer sows many seeds upon the ground and plants a multitude of seedlings, and yet not all that have been sown will come up in due season, and not all that were planted will take root, so also those who have been sown in the world will not all be saved." The version of the parable of the sower in the Gospel of Thomas does not similarly particularize and stress the seed that fails. But the motif of election versus rejection, with reference to the individual souls and apart from an historical or covenant community, is implicit in the gnostic context. Cf. Log. 23, "Jesus said: I shall choose you, one out of a thousand," and 62, "Jesus said, I tell my mysteries to those who are worthy of my mysteries."

polemic occasion or topos of debate in Jesus' ministry into which one can fit the saying. But he was speaking beyond any such ad hoc juncture to the dilemma of his people and the hope of Israel.

VI. IT WILL FOREVER KEEP
ITS FRESHNESS

I have been concerned first of all to insist on a naive reading of the parable. It must be allowed to speak for itself, and to go on *telling* from depth to depth. As Frost said of the genre of the poem, "Read it a hundred times: it will forever keep its freshness as a petal keeps its fragrance. It can never lose its sense of a meaning that once unfolded by surprise as it went." So the parable should be allowed to evoke its own horizon and its meaning in that horizon, independently of its interpreters. It should be allowed to awaken its own corresponding registers in our hearing, and even to create these. In this untrammeled exposure to it, we are captured by the primordial wonder that existence emerges out of, and prevails over, nothingness.

But I have also been concerned to inquire as to the structures of language and the structures of consciousness which make possible such communication. Such clarification of language and its operation refines and corrects our usual tools and methods of interpretation.

It is only to be added that this kind of study opens up access to the historical Jesus and to the Gospel in ways that carry a new kind of cogency. It is a question of a new or refined optic. The parable witnesses to Jesus *in its own way,* and to the concrete language-world which conditioned his proclamation and fate.

The bearing of this study of a parable upon other New Testament forms may be suggested by brief attention to the miracle story, or paradigm. Here, too, we have, as it were, the Gospel in miniature; here, too, its eschatological horizon and reality come to speech. In this "form," saving operation evoking astonishment over against impediment and limitation matches the scenario of the parable. As compared with a novelle or "legend," the economy and density of the language correspond to the "autonomy" of the parable form. In both cases, the gestalt effects "distance," excludes any immediate or conventional reference (or "through-meaning"), and therefore lights up a wider reality. The paradigm has power because, as in the case of the parable, its realism has gone through a sea-change. The medium dynamizes the content. A diurnal episode becomes a hierophany.

This is not to say that a novelle or "legend" (or, in the case of a parable, a secondary allegorizing interpretation) may not also "signal" a like revolution of expectation. I have cited one example of this in the case of the Peter-legend of the miraculous draught of fishes. But in such cases we see the community relating the basic model to its own history, or, in the case of the novelle, to popular propaganda styles.

From the point of view of linguistics, it is important to insist that the interpretation of a parable or a miracle story must go beyond ideational, theological, moral, or historical concerns, which are all reductionist. The import of the text is inseparably related to the "machinery" of its language, not only semantic, but lexical, grammatical, and syntactical. All such formalisms and codes go back into the oldest history of human speech and consciousness and subserve new communication. It is their operation in the text which establishes the public reality of what is spoken and authenticates the "world" which is evoked. The naive auditor responds to these subtle signals, but it is the task of the interpreter to penetrate and understand their operations.

II

THE SYMBOLICS OF JESUS
AND THE WAR
OF MYTHS

4

Jesus and the War
of Myths

I. SYMBOLIC LANGUAGE IN THE
NEW TESTAMENT

Any study of the language and rhetoric of a period must take account not
only of genres and styles, but also of the imagery that may be characteristic. Writers of different settings differ in their symbol and in their mythopoesis, as in other aspects of speech and communication. Here, too, fundamental apperception discloses itself. Reality as it is experienced in any
time is defined by the scope and repertory of its language, and not least by
those larger dramatizations of existence which are part of it.

Our present interest, therefore, is in the symbolic imagination as it evidences itself in the New Testament and the structures of its vision, a main
feature of which, no doubt, is related to its eschatological outlook. Peoples
and epochs see their respective worlds each in a different lighting, and this
governs their arts and all aspects of their creativity. In the title of this
second part of the book, I speak not of the symbolism, but of the
symbolics of Jesus. This term is intended to point to something more than
the images themselves. It is meant to suggest the social-psychological dimension of the symbol and the whole domain of cultural dynamics.

My topic, therefore, introduces us not to the imagery, but to the deeper
determinants which have shaped it and lent it power. Here we find ourselves in that unclarified domain associated with myths and archetypes.
No study of literature can ignore this dimension of meaning in language.
Yet the terms *myth* and *archetype* are used differently in different disciplines and contexts. It is enough here to recognize that there are deeper
structures in consciousness as well as the unconscious, the legacies of
our cultural past, varying in different cultures, dynamic patterns, which,

as Denis de Rougemont has said, "preform the inner movements of our sensibility."[1]

The affective and cognitive realities so crystallized "dictate—unknown to the authors—the profound rhetorics of their composition."[2]

DeRougemont has in mind such deeply embedded cultural "models" in our Western inheritance as those of Tristan, Don Juan, and Faust. His studies of love in the Western world have shown how such "archetypes" shape literary forms and the "action of language itself."[3] Not only so, but his canvass of the vicissitudes of such dynamic images and their literary expression bring to light the deeper theater of moral transformations in a society.

But we may extend his method as applied to these more recent images to include older and even more fateful patterns and archetypes associated with the Scriptures. Here, too, there are potent legacies in the Western soul which have determined its sense of reality and shaped the rhetorics of its creativity. Any study of the crisis of culture and of language today must take account of the vicissitudes of these residual, and still powerful, structures and syndromes as elements in our contemporary "crucible of images."

Surely one legitimate aim of literary criticism is to contribute to an understanding of our contemporary disorders at the level of the imagination. The student of the arts as we know them today cannot but be concerned with the related domain of cultural dynamics and with the sources and vehicles of cultural renewal. The theological critic, especially, will be impelled to explore the biblical archetypes and the ways in which they have shaped language and life. As biblical narrative can serve as a test for modern narrative, so biblical symbolics can offer a base from which we can better assess the special features and limitations of our modern sensibility.

In chapter 1, I called attention to that aspect of the Old Testament storytelling which required a total mythological world-plot and which related it to temporal existence and empirical reality. The present topic gives me an opportunity to explore further this holistic scope of the biblical epiphanies and their plastic media. My chief attention here will be given to the New Testament. What is said about the power and continuities of the biblical mythos, its social role, and its transformations in times of crisis like our own, will further document the resources of a theological criticism.

1. *Love Declared: Essays on the Myths of Love* (New York: 1963), p. 17.
2. Ibid., p. 44.
3. Ibid., p. 19.

II. MYTH AND VISION IN THE
NEW TESTAMENT

I shall order this discussion of the symbolic imagination of the New Testament about the terms *myth* and *vision*.[4] Both point us to the depth of sensibility and creativity with which we are concerned.

At least two phases of the discussion of myth in New Testament criticism have already been worked through. The older Christ-myth thesis of Drewes and others has long been obsolete. The more recent major discussion centering in Bultmann's work, of the "demythologizing" of the New Testament can be really fresh today only if the term *myth* is understood in a less technical sense than Bultmann understood it. More justice should be done to its mythopoetic character and its implicit claim to provide valid representation of the world and dramatization of existence. The Christian Scripture is full of myth in this sense. We can therefore pass over the fact that the actual word for myth, the Greek term *mythos,* occurs only five times in the latest writings of the canon, always in the pejorative sense of heretical fables or old wives' tales.[5]

So far as vision is concerned, the particular category of *dream* can be briefly set aside. The vocabulary of dream and dream phenomena is more abundant and diversified in our writings than is the case with myth. In most cases, the usages are predictable in these kinds of subliterary texts in this period. To associate guidance with dreams was traditional in both the Hebraic and pagan worlds, and narrative style employed this idea as a cliché. Even in more significant instances, as when Paul's campaign is directed across the Bosphorus into Europe by his dream of a man of Macedonia who bids him "come over to Macedonia and help us" (Acts 16:9), the interest is in the instruction, rather than the psychic state through which it was mediated. Nor do we have in such cases an enigmatic oracle requiring interpretation. In fact, dream interpretation (as distinguished from explanation of visions) is totally lacking in the New Testament. Though God himself is hidden, he "does not speak ambiguously. He wills to be understood."[6] "No New Testament witness thought

4. For a wider phenomenological treatment of these terms and the whole question of cultural dynamics, see the symposium volume entitled *Myths, Dreams, and Religion* (New York: E. P. Dutton, 1970), edited by Joseph Campbell for the Society for the Arts, Religion, and Contemporary Culture, New York.

5. For example, in 1 Timothy Christian teachers are charged not to "occupy themselves with myths and endless genealogies which promote speculations rather than divine training" (1:4), and again, "Having nothing to do with godless and silly myths" (4:7).

of basing the central message, the Gospel, or any essential part of it, on dreams."[7] This parsimony of dream phenomena corresponds to a main trend in late Second Temple Judaism and contrasts with the luxuriant picture in contemporary Hellenism, and even with the revival of such motifs in the rabbinic tradition.

What I have said so far bears on the dream in the strict sense of a disclosure in sleep. On the other hand, the New Testament vocabulary for *vision,* whether in a waking state or "by night," is very much more abundant and significant. The canon is full of visions and auditions, and this points to what is of main interest to us, the deeper dynamics of our human awareness. Actually, the most significant use in the New Testament of the Greek term for dream, *onar,* is one where it is in parallel with one of the terms for vision, *norasis,* as quoted in the Book of Acts from the prophet Joel:

> And your young men shall see visions,
> and your old men shall dream dreams (Acts 2:17).

This passage is part of Peter's discourse at the first Pentecost, and is typical in that it has to do with vision of the last things.

We make a fundamental observation here when we say that myth and dream in Christian Scripture are shaped by the eschatological consciousness. All the creative symbol is governed by the sense of world-transformation in course and of ultimate goals within reach, and these are social and cosmic goals, as well as individual. The entire Book of Revelation illustrates this. This work comprises a series of visions and auditions in the wider frame of a single unveiling or *apokalypsis* accorded to the author, and which he "saw" on the island of Patmos when he "was in the spirit on the Lord's day." Though the category of vision here is in the main a literary convention, and though the mythological material that fills the book is in good part compositional borrowing, yet the entire work is a *mythopoetic* reading of the contemporary experience of the community. It is an example of what we would call surrealism, animated by that sense of total crisis and world-metamorphosis which characterized the beginnings of Christianity throughout.

Our topic has already led us into a recognition of the large place in the New Testament of what the psychology of religion would call supranormal, ecstatic, and mystical experience. A list would include not only dreams,

---

6. G. Kittel, S. V. ed. *Theologische Wörterbuch zum Neuen Testament* (Stuttgart: Kohlhammer Verlag) (*Theological Dictionary of the New Testament,* tr. G. Bromley [Grand Rapids: Eerdmans, 1967], 5:220ff.)
7. Ibid., 5:235.

visions, and auditions, along with related trances, epiphanies, and theophanies, but also glossolalia, or "speaking in tongues" (which could be understood as the language of angels), raptures to heaven, and reports of various, quasi-magical transactions. Sometimes we find ourselves in a world of spells and archaic mentality. When Jesus gives a new name to Peter or to the sons of Zebedee, we recognize the archaic idea evidenced, for example, among the ancient Arabians, that the sheik had the power to change both the name and the nature of a tribesman. The primitive power of the spoken word appears again in the charismatic salutation of "peace" spoken by Jesus' disciples as they journeyed as heralds through the villages, a word which, if it is not accepted, returns to the speaker and leaves the hearers exposed to evil powers. Or this potency of speech can take the form of ritual doom-pronouncement, as in the legend of the death of Ananias and his wife.

An interesting example of what we would call levitation occurs in the account of Jesus walking on the sea. The variety of the three accounts in the Gospels makes it possible to trace the legend from its most developed form back to a more primitive stage. The oldest form may well be recognizable in the Gospel of John. Jesus here *appears* to the disciples distressed at night in their rowing, to reassure them. It is not said that they actually received him into the boat. The sequel of his manifestation is rather that "immediately the boat was at the land to which they were going." What we have here, as Rudolf Otto says, is "not a mere miracle as such but the quite definite category of an *apparitio,* and especially that of the charismatic figure who in hours of need and of mortal danger appears from afar in phantom form and gives help."[8] The episode is then transformed, first in Mark, where Jesus as really present enters the boat, and further in Matthew, where Peter also makes the attempt to walk on the water. Thus in both these later versions the memory of an apparition is carried over into the category of a levitation, one which also has abundant illustration in the history of religion. Otto's confidence in the historicity of the original apparition to the disciples need not be accepted, but his documentation suggests the cultural background in which these kinds of reports and their elaboration could take place. Quasi-telepathic conceptions, as of action at a distance, are clearly exemplified in Paul's relation to the church at Corinth. Though he is writing from across the Aegean with respect to a case of discipline, he assures the church that he will be present when, with the Holy Spirit, it carries out a formal act of excom-

8. *The Kingdom of God and the Son of Man,* tr. F. Filson and B. Lee-Woolf (Grand Rapids, Mich., 1938), p. 370.

munication against the offender, an action thought of realistically as carrying with it probable death.

As I have indicated, all these kinds of motifs and their narrative genres are predictable in popular writings of this period. But the early Christian movement arose from such depths that it was indeed accompanied by many kinds of charismatic and psychic phenomena, so much so that discrimination among them became a prior concern. Such supranormal experience was commonly assigned to the Spirit, that is, the Spirit of God, but some of its operations were more significant than others, and there were also false spirits. In the Corinthian church, for example, Paul was confronted with a veritable riot of ecstatic manifestations associated with Gnostic or related ideas and with antinomian ethics. He discusses all this under the head of "visions and revelations." He himself, he observes, is as much an initiate as anyone with respect to "spiritual gifts." In fact, either in or out of the body, he says, he had been caught up to the third heaven and heard forbidden matters. But, he insists, it is nothing to boast of and leads to fantasies of false transcendence, unless subordinated to down-to-earth responsibility, as in the case of Christ himself.

With respect to Jesus, I would agree with the view that he can be called a *charismatic*.[9] The category of *mystic* varies so in different contexts that it should be used of Jesus only in the most guarded way. Certainly if it implies emphasis on a psychological state for its own sake or the use of special techniques and disciplines for the attainment of such a state, it does not apply to him. Yet in the case of Jesus, as in that of St. Francis, we have an interesting example of the seer with visionary sensibility who is at the same time a clear-headed realist. He sees the connection of prodigious matters in the twinkling of an eye and can crystallize such vision in a parable or metaphor of the utmost simplicity. In this connection, it should be borne in mind that the accounts in the Gospels of certain of his visions, such as those ascribed to him on the occasions of his baptism and his temptation, as well as the vision seen by the three disciples on the Mount of Transfiguration, have been extensively reworked by the tradition. Yet these instances, as well as the epiphanies reported in the Gospels recounting his resurrection appearances, testify to both the dynamic power of the movement that began with him and to the momentous mythopoetic language it called forth.

To conclude this section, we can summarize, saying that the Christian

9. See the author's *Eschatology and Ethics in the Teaching of Jesus,* rev. ed. (New York: Harpers, 1950), chap. 12, especially pp. 202–14.

Scripture gives us a wide documentation on dreams, visions, and associated media of revelation and wisdom. The styles and literary forms reflect
these deeper dynamics. Our writings confirm the importance of the prerational dimension in human experience. But the modes and conditions of
such phenomena are not dealt with in any sophisticated way. Their origin
and operation are referred to the Spirit of God, and their import is construed in terms of the message and mythos of the movement, which, of
course, had its taproot in the history of Israel.

III. THE CARNAL AND DUSTY BONDS
OF CHRISTIAN MYTH

> Unique and individual perceptions require to be
> "grounded," in both the ontological and electrical senses
> of the metaphor "ground." . . . If there is anything to the
> master Christian images, it is a carnal and dusty bond we
> have with historical universality; as it is in flesh of our
> flesh and bone of our bone that God has put in potency
> before us what it is to be before him as his man.
>
> Ray L. Hart, *Unfinished Man and the Imagination*

We turn now to look in more detail at the category of myths and mythopoetic representation. One feature of Christian Scripture that is significant
for our wider critical undertaking is the continuity of its mythos from
ancient times. We have a prime example here of the stubbornness of social
symbol through cultural change, the time-binding character of such symbol,
and the way in which it provides coherence to human society. This may
be recognized despite the mutations it undergoes, as, for example, in the
transition from Judaism to Christianity. It is as if a kind of lifeline of
meaning and orientation ran through the millenniums, identified with the
oldest Hebrew archetypes. This is all the more remarkable when we note
the survival of these images and ritual motifs down into the present day.
The political imagery of divine kingship and covenant which underlies
Jewish and Christian worship today goes back even beyond the Hebraic
foundations to the ancient Near East. No doubt there was a radical recon-
ception of the old Hittite and Mesopotamian antecedents by Israel, as
there was of Jewish and Greco-Roman antecedents in the rise of Christianity. But there is an underground continuity, as is evident in the Scripture
itself.

To know the way of life of a people or a society, one must enter into
its myth and dream, its folklore and its art. To know about political doc-

trine alone, or social ideology, is not enough. The same holds true for understanding a religious community and its faith. The dogma or the confession tells only half the story, that part of it which separates and stresses discontinuity. One can illustrate from the Old Testament. Scholars have identified in the Pentateuch an ancient confessional formula which they call the "credo of Israel." Here Israel's origin, its "adoption," is connected with the events of the Exodus from Egypt. This credo served to establish the identity of this people and its loyalties as against other cultures. But the deeper connections of Israel with all mankind come to expression in a rich mythos of origins, also in the Pentateuch, and in the Psalms and the prophets.[10] The iconoclasm of Israel always remains indebted to its antecedents in the ancient Orient.[11]

The same consideration holds for the apparently discontinuous character of the corresponding New Testament credo or kerygma and its all but exclusive focus on Christ. Essential as it is for Christian self-understanding, it is only an abbreviated pointer to the faith. By overemphasis on it, theologians isolate the Gospel in its origins from both Judaism and paganism. The deeper richness of the Christian consciousness in that period and its continuities with the past are recognized only when we enter into the mythical legacies with which the kerygma clothed itself. Again, the iconoclasm of Christianity always remains indebted to its antecedents and rivals. It is only so that it could ever make any claim to universality.

But there is one further point here. The long lineage of early Christian

10. To give one example, I cite Isa. 51:9–11. Here the deliverance of Israel at the Red Sea is colored with ancient pre-Israelitic creation-myth, that of the slaying of the dragon and the establishment of world order. These overtones in the rehearsal of Israel's election are invoked to convey the full meaning of the eschatological fulfillment now promised to the exiles returning from the captivity.

> Was it not thou that didst cut Rahab in pieces,
> that didst pierce the dragon?
> Was it not thou that didst dry up the sea,
> the waters of the great deep?

11. "One aspect of the dynamic which animates the universe of mythic representations [is the iconoclastic]. This iconoclastic tendency appears whenever history occasions a confrontation of rival symbolisms. This conflict leads to refusals and pitiless exclusions; it also brings about reciprocal enrichments. In the Old Testament the conflict of symbol with symbol attaches itself to the interpretation of the history of Israel as a history of salvation. It transforms that history in a 'crucible of symbolization,' a crucible which appropriates from the religious universe of the civilizations which surround Israel representations which it demythicizes, and others which remythicize the history of Israel. This recovery of archaic symbols, whether obsolete or still surviving, takes place most often thanks to retrospective interpretation of the ancient symbolic language in the light of a new 'experience of the sacred.' Pierre Barthel, *Interprétation du language mythique et theologie biblique* (Leiden, 1963), pp. 298–99 (summarizing a section of Paul Ricoeur's "La Symbolique du mal" [see n. 14]).

myth back through the centuries and millenniums says something about its contact with humanness and secularity. The first Christian imagination, myth, and vision had archaic roots in the life of mankind and direct relation to the most ancient epiphanies. If this was true historically, on the horizontal plane of time, it was also true phenomenologically, vertically, in the individual. Indeed, Paul Ricoeur has shown how the New Testament symbolics of evil and purgation include psychic strata which go down into primordial human categories. He notes that only the long way back of reflection on the successive layers of the great cultural symbols can match psychoanalysis and cooperate with its regressive exploration.[12]

Mythical motifs in the New Testament having a long prehistory can be further illustrated. Let us take, for example, the Christmas story. The birth of the Divine Child, the discovery of his hidden birthplace by the humble, his persecution by the usurper, his inauguration of the Golden Age; for these elements in the nativity stories of Christ, the Gospels draw on worldwide myth and folklore. Note especially the analogies to the birth of Horus and to Vergil's Fourth Eclogue. The version of the nativity that we find in the twelfth chapter of the Book of Revelation sets it in a cosmological drama that goes back to old solar myth and the primeval war with the dragon. In this case, all such myth and vision is now transparently related to actual events in the Roman provinces and reordered to interpret the birth of Christ, his being "caught up to God and his throne," and the persecution of his church. Thus always the poet uses old archetypes and symbol to inform present experience.

All such dynamic imagery in the New Testament has this vital relation to situations and events. It is not merely decorative, literary, or freefloating. Moreover, what is borrowed becomes both old and new. It is new because it is used in a new system of symbols and because it is related to this particular history. Even such a general archetype as death and rebirth takes on a stubbornly different meaning, as in fact it does in every culture. The various vegetation cults of the ancient Mediterranean and Near Eastern world were all very different, as Henri Frankfort has shown. Where the church adopted pagan or Hellenistic motifs like that of the Divine Child, or those associated with the sacred meal, or such images as those of Dionysus turning water into wine, these elements are all transformed by the power of the new myth. Yet there is a continuity.

I cannot leave this theme of the continuity of a Christian myth without noting the problem created today by the radical discontinuity in our own

12. "The Hermeneutics of Symbols and Philosophical Reflection," *International Philosophical Quarterly* 2 (1962):195.

cultural crisis. The modern arts widely reflect a sensibility which not only disowns symbolic legacies, but prizes immediate atomistic perception without interpretation, "happenings," the unrelated epiphany, emancipation from sequence of any kind. There is hardly any parallel in the past to this extreme revolt, even in the age of the Sophists or in the solipsism of the Romantic movement on the Continent. Gnosticism's world-loathing still had its myth, its house of being. No doubt we should understand the present atomization and "dry mock" of all ordering symbol as a ruthless testing of reality, pushed to the limit, to be followed by a reconstruction of authentic structures. After all, the human body has its stable form, and the human psyche is no less stubborn in its basic gestalt. There is in it something which resists any such radical change of consciousness as would constitute mania or chaotic phantasmagoria. Therefore it appears to me that those very ancient structures of consciousness that have provided orientation and stability for man in existence and have served as a kind of lifeline of order and survival will again reassert themselves.

IV. THE WAR OF MYTHS

I have tried to show in the preceding section that our early Christian texts provide us with an example of the long continuity of myth through cultural changes. But they also document what happens to myth in a time of crisis, and this should be of special interest to all of us in our modern situation. In the first century, both Judaism and paganism were passing through a radical challenge, and the emerging church was caught up in the creativity on both sides and in the war of myths of the period. The early believers represented an eschatological sect of Judaism, and continued Judaism's ancient war on pagan myths, idols, and rites. Yet it also developed powerful imagery drawn from Jewish apocalyptic, from Jewish-Hellenistic syncretism, and from the dualistic and gnostic impulse in paganism. We see continuity and discontinuity throughout, mythoclasm and mythoplasm.

In a time of crisis like this, a new mythical impulse or mythopoesis is engaged on two fronts. It has to speak to the situation of the loss of roots, the faded myth, anomie. But this brings it into conflict with social authority and establishment. We see both aspects in the Christian Scripture.

1. Mythopoeic Impulse in a Situation of Faded Myth and Anomie.

We have an example of this in the explosion of the Christian eschatological myth and its community-building power in the disarray of the Hellenistic world. The new faith arose out of a momentous epiphany in the first-century world, and its creativity was manifest in a wealth of dramatic imagery which answered to the prevailing hungers. The astonishing prestige of the gnostic fabulations in this period is a parallel phenomenon, and its relation to the Hellenistic anomie has been impressively set forth by Hans Jonas. At this time, the ideology of the Greek polis had long been in trouble and, as today, the masses craved for some new crystallization of meaning and community.

The Christian movement related itself to the unconscious dynamics of the time, and so created a new language, or rather metamorphosed the existing rhetorics, styles, and symbolics. We have here an example of what has been called a *language-event,* that is, an epochal revolution in the gamut and power of language, including new imagery, a liberation of human speech, and a new grasp on reality. Such a mutation cannot be explained, but it is helpful to use the tools of social psychology. It is evident at least, that the psychic structures or archetypes of a long past had broken down, together with their symbols. The new Christian myth and dream met the situation by both rejection and appropriation. Old dream was quickened at a greater depth, thanks to a new experience of the holy.

I have cited the dynamic motif of the birth of the Divine Child, known throughout the Mediterranean world in diverse forms. I could also illustrate by the old cultural image of the hero-deliverer or divine man (*theios anēr*), typically represented by Hercules and his legend, many of whose traits were later absorbed into the portrayal of Christ. Or I could point to the whole phenomenology of rebirth and renewal in the pagan world. All such legacies were now quickened from the depths by the Christian mythopoesis, unified about a center, and publicized in rhetorics both celebrative and narrative which engaged with the contemporary idiom and sensibility. As the great classicist Wilamovitz observed with reference to the long decay of the language of the Greeks, and speaking of Paul, "At last someone speaks in Greek out of a fresh inward experience in life," though to Paul "all literature is a bauble."[13] It is worth noting by way of comparison that Tannaitic Judaism, in that phase in which it prosecuted a mission to the Gentiles, entered into no such radical and dangerous encounter with the psychic structures of paganism. Where some forms of speculative and heretical Judaism did so, their venture into syncretism failed either to safeguard the Hebraic roots or to renew the classical inheritance. The Christian church did both, and laid the basis for a new world order in the Empire.

One question that always haunts any discussion of myths is that of

13. *Die griechische und lateinische Literatur und Sprache* (Berlin, 195), p. 157.

"broken myth," and the disparity between genuine primordial epiphany, with its irrecoverable naivete, and "myth" in such a relatively advanced culture as that of the first century. Civilized man, we are told, is forever debarred by his *"oubli du sacré"* from this kind of autonomous mentality. It is true that when we speak of the mythological elements in the New Testament, we have to do with much that has passed from the state of genuine archaic myth into that of culturized symbol—whether democratized myth, or historicized myth, or even folklore or literary allusion. Nevertheless, the true epiphanic and ecstatic potential survives in mankind and is creative, world-creative, in given situations. The power of such an impulse in the midst of first-century Judaism and Hellenism related it to primordial epiphany and was such as to organize many forms of secondary myth into a unified vision corresponding to its similarly fashioned ritual.

What holds true for the Christian impact on Hellenism also applies to the beginning in Galilee. In this case, the situation of faded myth and anomie refers not to Judaism as a whole at the time of the ministry of Jesus, but to the disoriented groups suggested by the term *sinners* in the Gospels. For them, the meaning of the inherited patterns of Jewish life and their sanctions had been eroded by social changes. They lived on the margin of the official cultus and of the movement of restoration represented by the synagogue and the Pharisees. The vigor of the eschatological groups in this period, including the sect which left us the Dead Sea scrolls, testifies both to disaffection with the existing authorities and the impulse to renewal.

The power of Jesus' initiative among the unchurched groups was inseparable from the dramatizations he employed. His language drew on old archetypes and more recent imagery in such a way as to ignite the dream and incentives of his relatively few followers. It was only secondarily that Jesus found himself at odds with the official orthodoxy and those circles for whom traditional images were still vital. The death of Jesus, as a famous poem of Allen Tate ("The Cross") suggests, threw a blinding light on what was at stake, and inevitably led to a situation that resembled a war of myths, though it was a conflict within Israel still. But this leads to the other aspect of which I have spoken.

2. *Mythopoeic Impulse and Social Authority.*

Myth-making in the rise of Christianity not only met the problem of the breakdown of older myth, but inevitably entered into conflict with existing authority. I note this first as regards what we can call the "establishment" in the Roman Empire and its cities. This war of myths is dramatically orchestrated in the Book of Revelation, with a full repertory of ancient cosmological motifs. We have here something like a cosmic opera whose dramatis personae include all the powers and agencies in heaven and earth and whose plot is conceived in the tradition of the holy war. Though we shrink from the gory detail and the unfairness to the humanistic values of Rome at its best, yet we should recognize what is at stake in these surreal tableaux. The eighteenth chapter contains a list of the products exchanged by the merchants in this great emporium, Rome, the new Babylon: cargoes of "gold, silver, jewels and pearls," all "articles of ivory, all articles of costly wood, bronze, iron and marble," also incense, spices, wine, oil, fine flour and wheat, cattle and sheep, horses and chariots, and finally, "bodies" (that is, slaves) and "human souls." The items in this list are taken mainly from the famous taunt-song against Tyre in the prophet Ezekiel. The Greek translation of Ezek. 27:13 reads, "Hellas and the regions about traded with you for the souls of men." But the Book of Revelation has set all these same wares in an ascending series, with this as the climax. Sir William Walton, the composer, has used this climax with tremendous effect in his oratorio *Belshazzar's Feast*.

This example shows that where primitive Christianity became involved in a war of myths, issues like human slavery were at stake. This goes right back to Jesus, who said, "Of how much more value is a man than a sheep" (Matt. 12:12). Surely any myth and dream of any age or inspiration must finally be answerable to this kind of test.

I turn now from the conflict of early Christian myth with paganism to its conflict with Judaism, beginning with Jesus himself. This is usually presented as a conflict over the Jewish law and is, of course, a highly sensitive and controversial topic. But we can, at least, seek to go behind the usual terms of the discussion. Whether as regards Jesus or Paul, the issue as to the law can be illuminated if studied as one example of a crisis in social symbols and archetypes. Normative Judaism in Jesus' day was dealing with this problem in one way and certainly safeguarded much of the cultural dynamics of the tradition. In this same crisis, Jesus and his followers selected differently out of Israel's past, both conscious and unconscious, impelled by a new and momentous epiphany or experience of the sacred. Both movements felt themselves to be faithful to the law and the covenants. But each related itself differently to the deeper structure of the past, and this meant different ways of dealing with the present.

I can present this divergence in two ways. At the level of imagery, one can show that Jesus of Nazareth reordered the symbolic and mythical legacies of Israel and established new priorities, especially by a leap back to the oldest covenant imagery, especially the covenant of creation. In the second place, at a level that underlies the first and that requires the use of social-psychological tools, one can show that Jesus dealt more fundamentally than his contemporaries with the deeper strata of human existence. For this second level, I refer to the phenomenological study by Paul Ricoeur of what one can best call the *psychodynamics* of the ancient world, including the period with which we are concerned.[14]

Ricoeur's phenomenological study of the issues with which I have been engaged in this chapter is carried out in the context of his wider investigation of the evolution of man's moral consciousness, especially in the part entitled *The Symbolism of Evil*. By the first century of our era, Israel, like pagan antiquity, had long passed through the two earliest stages of man's sense of rift or alienation from the order of the sacred, each stage with its own strategies of expiation. The first stage was that in which his unrest was alone identified by such nonmoral symbols as stain or impurity or infection calling for cleansing. Survivals of this stage are reflected in texts of confession from the oldest cultural records we possess. The second stage, also very old, corresponds to a new level of culture in which we have a communal consciousness of sin as deviation from the order of things or group offense against God or the gods,all suggested by symbols of bondage or possession and calling for deliverance or atonement. Language of the earlier stage is carried along into the new. The value of those ancient symbols was that they recognize that evil is a part of the history of being, and of social being. Evil is already there, is not the opposite of good; it has an external aspect or is an enslaving power that cannot be dealt with by the will alone.

But by the time with which we are concerned, Israel, like Greece, had long passed to a third stage, that of the interiorized guilt of the individual, evoking images now first of all not of stain or sin, but of burden. In the Old Testament as a whole, the deeper sensibilities of evil as a mystery had been carried over into this third stage. But before the common era, this depth became attenuated with a new focus on the individual and his obligation to the law, the latter now taking on an increasingly juridical character. Thus we can understand the structuring of the Judaism of our period about this third stage, and the categories of law, transgression, obedience,

    14. *Philosophie de la volunté*, pt. 2, *Finitude et culpabilité* (Paris: 1960), vol. 2, "La Symbolique du mal," with its two sections "The Primary Symbols: Stain, Sin, Guilt" and "The Myths of Origins and End." See also Barthel, *Interprétation*, chap. 5, "L'Interprétation symbolique des représentations d'origine et de structure mythiques par Paul Ricoeur." (An English edition of Ricoeur is available, *The Symbolism of Evil*, tr. E. Buchanon [Boston: Beacon Press, 1967]).

repentance, gratitude, reward. The Pharisees carried through their admirable ethico-juristic and casuistic program enriched by the Haggadah, and the ethics of the people, with its emphasis on freedom and responsibility, was the loftiest in the world of that time. Yet in terms of cultural anthropology, it was the ethic of an epoch, and it was now in crisis, as we can see by the diverging sectarian movements and circles identified with apocalyptic visionaries or wisdom speculation. Like the mythology of the Enlightenment in our modern period, the symbolics of this stream of Judaism had forfeited connection, to some degree, with the earlier strata of man's experience of evil, including the preethical and prerational. Thus Ricoeur can ask whether the "will to complete and exact obedience, even sustained by the joyous acceptance of a grateful heart, carries over fully the God-relation expressed earlier in the conjugal symbolism of the prophets."[15] And he asks whether the spiritual regime of the law espoused by the Jewish teachers "could recognize its own abysses."[16]

It is to be remembered that such an analysis is proposed not at a theological level but a phenomenological. A comparative study of the symbolics of evil is carried out to throw light on the deeper structures of meaning and the role of cultural myth. It is suggested that the imagery of Jesus represented in part a recovery of older archetypes, especially of those evoking the "nonethical face of evil," thus demoralizing the patterns of his day. That Paul should focus so much of his debate with Jewish opponents upon the theme of justification shows that he too found himself necessarily dealing with the Judaism of this particular epoch. His preferred Jewish categories and symbols drew on older levels of Israel's consciousness. In conclusion, lest Ricoeur's study appear partisan, it should be noted that his method can disclose analogous vicissitudes, or what he calls *gauchissements,* in other religious traditions, including those of Christianity.

The focal image of Jesus' message was that of the Kingdom of God, viewed as imminent and constituting both grace and total demand. It is not enough to say that Jesus goes back to the prophets. The ultimate reference of his message and vision is that of the creation itself. This is suggested by the cosmic-eschatological character of the Kingdom which he announced, in this respect different from the eschatology of the Pharisees associated with the age to come and the national hope. It partakes of the total Alpha-Omega scope of apocalyptic, without its curiosities and phantasmagoria. Jesus identified the opposition to the Kingdom with Satan and the demons,

15. *La Symbolique du mal,* p. 129.
16. Ibid., p. 134.

and this central symbolism confirms the creation archetype. It is as though for Jesus many of the intervening cultural strata in Judaism, with their long sedimentation of social and psychic habit, had collapsed like so many floors. We may take as illustrative his appeal back of Moses to the "beginning of creation" in the words assigned to him in the dispute with the Jewish teachers about divorce (Mark 10:6). Jesus' attitude to moral evil was one that recognized its ambiguity and its close relation to possession, one of Ricoeur's archaic symbols for the experience of alienation.

This depth in the sanctions of Jesus explains the implicit universalism in his position, as in his attitude to the Samaritans; his attitude to nature and the creatures (for example, the flowers of the field and the birds of the air); his appeals to reason, common sense, and the processes of nature; and the quasi-secular tone of his parables and much of his teaching.[17] I am not saying that Jesus reverted to the creation motif alone, but that his imagery met the current dilemma by reordering all its symbolics in depth. One aspect of this is the convergence in him of the various roles and styles of the three main types of Israel's spokesmen—prophet, sage, and scribe.

I have been speaking in this section about the conflict of a new mythical impulse with social authority and illustrating it in the case of Jesus. Jesus went behind the particular symbol structure of his time, and this meant a critique of the law as then understood and its patterns both in the unconscious life and in public institutions. We have an example here of the restructuring of myth in close relation to social and cultural change. As the breach with the synagogue developed, we find that Jesus' use of the creation archetype is carried through. Paul's decisive framework is that of creation and new creation, just as his basic category for interpreting Christ is that of the new Adam. In the Gospels, the corresponding category is that of the Son of man. This image, with its apocalyptic and universal roots and implications, is related to that of the First Man and dominates the Gospel of Mark.[18] The Jewish category of Messiah is entirely subordinated to it, just as it played little role in Jesus' own imagery. It is important, however, to make clear that the revolution in images initiated by Jesus should not be viewed as a war of myths between Judaism and Christianity. The divergence then, as to this day, is within the same household

17. Cf. the author's "Equivalents of Natural Law in the Teaching of Jesus," *Journal of Religion* 26 (1946), pp. 125–35.

18. It is related to this that in Mark's account of the temptation of Jesus, the scene suggests Eden before the Fall: Jesus is in the company of angels and "wild beasts," the latter harmless in the Paradisal state. In this same setting, the first Adam fell; the second did not.

of faith. Not only Jesus, but also Paul, understood himself to be faithful to the law and the covenants. But it is of interest to note that that same radical appeal to older archetypes which occasioned the conflict with the parent faith made possible an effective encounter with the universe of symbols of the Gentile world.

V. THE CONCRETE UNIVERSALISM OF BIBLICAL MYTH

I have sought to discuss myth and dream in Christian Scripture in dynamic terms, rather than theological. We have found illustration here of the power of the mythopoetic impulse and some of its phenomena. We have concentrated upon the issues of continuity and discontinuity: the unbroken lifelines of older archetypes offering orientation to culture, yet the vicissitudes that such symbols underwent in the course of cultural change. There is, however, one feature of our material which requires a closing comment.

The myth and dream of Jewish and Christian origin is unique in its nexus with man's social experience and his historical life. This is a commonplace in all study of comparative religion. The most radical discontinuity we have had to recognize was that in which Hebraism historicized the older mythos of the ancient Near East. The new myth and ritual of Israel was oriented to time, to the birth of the people in time, and to its promise and obligation in time. The mythology of natural cycles was largely overcome. The Christian mythos, indeed, looked to the end of history, but in such a way that the historical experience of man was still validated.

All this has meant that, as against some other kinds of world vision, the Jewish and Christian myth has been inextricably involved in the pragmatic vicissitudes of the West, in its social and political, as well as cultural life, disaster as well as achievements. This means also that its original epiphanies and symbols have been often distorted, overlaid, and given false theoretic formulation. If our basic concern is with the problem of cultural dynamics today, the sources and vehicles of cultural renewal, it is important that this particular mythology should be dissociated from such distortions and understood in its origins and total context. To this end, the kind of social-psychological approach represented in this chapter can make a contribution.

In the foregoing discussion of the symbolics of the New Testament, I have had occasion at various points to suggest implications for contemporary literary assessment. If, as de Rougemont observes, inherited archetypes "preform the inner movements of our own sensibility" and even dictate "the profound rhetorics of our composition," we can well ask how far this is true today in the case of these once dynamic apperceptions. Their continuity through earlier vicissitudes has been noted, as well as their power for cultural order and literary creativity. What is fundamentally distinctive about their basic theophanies and their mythos is their concrete universalism. A teleology of the world-process is envisioned in inseparable relation to the moral dimension of personal existence in time with all its social realities. As we have insisted, this kind of ephiphany was one that required historization and embodiment, though not without its own forms of psychic and spiritual transcendence. Wherever in the classic period this vision of the world became involved in a war of myths, what was at stake was some such issue as that of human slavery. Here other visions and their rhetorics can be tested, including those of the present day.

5

The New Voice

I. SPEECH AS PRIMAL GESTURE

There are certain wider aspects of the texts of primitive Christianity and of their underlying tradition which we tend to overlook in our addiction to familiar tools and methods. Such new dimensions are brought to our attention commonly by labors in other disciplines. One such area is that of the wider phenomenology of speech or language, understood as a primal "gesture" of our species—a gesture of innumerable and Protean varieties and modulations; a gesture varying with numerous cultural factors and, not least, with a given sense of time.

Morphology in the arts has been analyzed with respect to particular space-time categories in particular cultures. H. M. and N. K. Chadwick have noted the correlation of rhetorical forms in early Indian literature with the special sense, or rather lack of sense for history, especially the absence of certain genres such as personal poetry and poetry of national interest in a given period.[1] Jakob Burckhardt already had noted the repugnance of Islam to the epic, attributed the absence of drama in this civilization to the dominant concept of fate, and drawn attention to the handicaps of drama in India.[2] The historical consciousness of a society or of one group in a society; the sense of past and future; the sense of cultural continuities or of cultural crisis—all these may vary exceedingly, and language in all its aspects will vary correspondingly.

Such variability in language appears not only in the presence or absence of particular genres or styles, not to mention vocabularies, but in very fundamental matters such as speech structure and grammar, and the relativity of these latter to basic presuppositions about time, space, etc., is under study in modern linguistics. Aspects of speech more immediately accessible to observation and relevant to our field of study would include

1. *The Growth of Literature* (1932–40), 2:460.
2. *Reflections on History* (London, 1943), pp. 89, 69.

the distinction between oral and written discourse, between the laconic and the prolix, between official or sacred conventions and popular or secular idiom. There are also deeper or primitive modes of utterance relative to cultural or existential factors whose role in a society or group may be indicative—such modes as exclamation, incantation, glossolalia, curse, spell, narrative, dialogue. Nor should we forget the wide gamut of differences with respect to the "self"-consciousness of speaker or author, from the anonymous voice of a group, through all the gradations of the "inspired" role, to this or that kind of individual sense of spokesmanship and "personality."

The older lives of Jesus, for example, most often rest upon a modernizing view of his selfhood in terms of autonomous individuality. One of the most interesting features of the "new quest" is the relocation of the reality of his person and identity, and therefore of his utterance, to accord with his eschatological involvement.[3] One could ask pertinent questions here as to the widely varying sense of individuality and self-understanding of various first-century figures, with special attention to their sense of time and history, and the bearing of this upon their patterns of speech or teaching: Hillel, the Baptist, a Qumran exegete, Jesus, Judas of Galilee, or the author of the Assumption of Moses.

There are, indeed, features of our early Christian texts which are alien to our usual categories and which may pass through the sieve of our assessment. We raise the question here particularly with respect to the underlying oral deposits. We have learned from Ernst Fuchs to look upon the eruption of the Gospel in Palestine as, among other things, a startling and novel event in the order of language, a *Sprachereignis,* a shock to the existing fabric of human discourse, the effects and reverberations of which were felt in many ways. When we consider how primal an activity speech is in the human being, and how deeply linked it is with all that identifies our very being and "world," we can recognize the momentousness of the new movement by its revolutionary manifestations in this domain. Whether language is seen in its psychological aspect, with von Humboldt, as an *energeia* (marvelling as he did at the stupendous luxuriance, the sheer volume of man's loquacity), or, more correctly as a *fait social* (Durkheim), the consequences for speech of the emerging Christian movement surely constitute a significant field of observation.

The emergence of this movement was a speech-event in two senses. More fundamentally, it was a speech-event (and in English, as has been

3. J. M. Robinson, *Kerygma und historischer Jesus* (1960), pp. 149ff.

observed, we should here translate *Sprachereignis* as "language-event")
in the sense that the meaningful content of knowing and of consciousness
itself were transformed and enlarged. But it was also a speech-event in the
sense that the various modes, registers, patterns, and forms of utterance
were modified or renewed. It brought with it "freedom of speech," in the
sense both of release from dumbness, sullenness, inhibition, and in the
sense of novelty, improvisation, and prodigality. Observations of these
kinds can be made with respect to the whole "speech-phenomenon" of the
New Testament period, whether oral or written, and without falling into
romanic categories ("eloquence," "afflatus," "sublime"). The occasion for
this novelty, after all, was eschatology, or, closely related to eschatology,
a kind of crisis in culture very different from those that have overthrown
one or another kind of formalism or classicism.

The sequel will show how much I am indebted to Ernst Fuchs for drawing attention to this whole matter of the *Sprachereignis* and *Sprachphä-
nomen* of the Gospel. It is to be borne in mind that he uses these terms in
an existentialist context which lends even greater significance to the realities in question. Here, for Fuchs, language and "historicness" (*Geschicht-
lichkeit*) are identified.[4] That is, our language is our "world" and our
reality, and not only in the usual sense ("The limits of my language are
the limits of my world"—Wittgenstein; or "Choose this or that language,
and change your image of the world"—Adam Schaff); but our language
is our world also in the sense of our concern, relationship, love. Our present discussion is directed for the most part to the novelty or distinctiveness
of the forms, genres, modes of speech in the Gospel, that is, to the rhetorical dimension, but always with the understanding that these may have a significance that leads to the heart of Gospel.

If we find one key to the special phenomenon of primitive Christian
speech in eschatology, we must still make distinctions. The eruption of
the new age no doubt meant a break in cultural continuities, including
those of such a fundamental matter as language, but the impact of this
factor could vary. Certainly the language-phenomena of the Qumran community, which were also conditioned by eschatology, differ from those of
the Gospel. The considerable role played by written texts, other than Scripture, both at Qumran and in Jewish apocalyptic circles, may be taken as

4. In a later essay, Professor Wilder was critical of Fuchs and Ebeling for think-
ing of the language-event in cultural, or even anticultural, terms. See Amos N.
Wilder, "The Word as Address and the Word as Meaning," in *New Frontiers in
Theology: Discussions Among Continental and American Theologians,* vol. 2, *The
New Hermeneutic,* ed. James M. Robinson and John B. Cobb, Jr. (New York:
Harper & Row, 1964), pp. 198–218—*ED.*

one example. Perhaps the more advanced eschatological timetable of Jesus and his immediate followers accounts for the exclusively oral character of their discourse and for other differences of their rhetoric. But the influence of eschatology upon the speech patterns of the Essenes and related groups, as upon those of the Christian movement, no doubt varied even within a short time.

The prophetic-apocalyptic ethos of the Christian community after Easter differed from the outlook of Jesus himself and conditioned a different kind of voice and tongue. As time passed, and as the church in this or that group began to look for the second coming, rather than for the one consummation, the changed eschatological consciousness reflected itself in correspondingly different speech patterns. In such later phases, indeed, we see the church taking over rhetorical forms from the synagogue or Qumran: school patterns or legal or hymnic styles, which the earlier acute eschatological consciousness had transcended. The changing sense of time and of history is as manifest in the modes and forms of Christian language as in its doctrine, and the two go together. In the course of this development, the Jesus-tradition, for example, was modified also in its formal and rhetorical aspects by these later phases. As the eschatological reality, for instance, became identified retrospectively with the person of Jesus, rather than (as by him) with the operation of God, in course, the style and tenor of his sayings were modified so that they took on a didactic or legislative character, and a similar impulse affected the narrative tradition and anecdotes. The peculiar features of the Gospel genre, as shaped by the author of Luke-Acts, are decisively conditioned by the author's understanding of time and history. But this same correlation holds for all aspects of the early Christian literature, not only for its written genres, but also for its preliterary elements.

In the present paper, we must confine ourselves to limited probings of our topic. We shall deal with 1) convention and novelty in the rhetorics of the Gospel, and 2) the significance of the oral mode of discourse in the case of Jesus and his followers.

II. CONVENTION AND NOVELTY

How far did the eschatological consciousness of the Gospel modify prevailing language patterns or even disrupt the continuities and conventions of the inherited rhetoric? Evidently, speech is a cultural phenomenon, as are the various speech forms and media of a society. There is a rather rigid, conventional aspect about common genres and veins of utterance, whether oral or written, whether intimate or official, whether forensic or cultic, whether paraenetic or narrative, whether hymn, oracle, or epistle. Yet all such aspects of language and communication change gradually, together with changes in experience and in the basic sense of existence. Changes may be imperceptible or sudden, but they affect the whole gamut of word and meaning: sensibility, images, speech forms, rhythm, vocabulary, and conceptuality. Any novelty cannot be totally iconoclastic, since articulation commonly presupposes a hearer. "Too rapid changes in language would make it defeat it own purpose," that is, communication. "What is usual in the history of the languages of the world is not change but stability."[5] Thus glossolalia, as an endpoint of disorder in speech, is either rejected by society as mania or saved for public meaning by some tour de force of interpretation.

The influence of a radical eschatological impulse in a society upon language is related to the larger issue as to time-sense and language generally. Alf Sommerfelt, writing on "Language, Society and Culture," discusses this larger topic. Evidently there are various correlations that can be made between the varying time-senses of different cultures and their tongues.

> Relativity is characteristic of the conception of time not only in different societies, but also within the same society. . . . It is not only that formal time-units are different in different societies, it is the concept of time itself and its importance in social life that differs. The special importance given to the time sequence in the western societies seems to be a particular trait which may be brought into relation with the characters of the verbal systems of the languages they speak.[6]

This order of considerations would raise the question of whether the radical iconoclasm of the Gospel affected Aramaic or Greek at the profound level, not of vocabulary or style, but of grammatical and syntactic structure. Setting this question aside, we shall attend to other aspects of speech which are also in their own way fundamental.

One can test the kind and degree of novelty of the new covenant over against the old in terms of the kind of language-phenomena with which we are concerned. We have here another measure of the break between Judaism and the Gospel, a measure of what was intended in the Christian theme of promise and fulfillment. Certainly the eschatology of Jesus and his first

5. A Sommerfelt, *Diachronic and Synchronic Aspects of Language* (The Hague, 1962), p. 109, citing A. Meillet.

6. Ibid., p. 122. The author also cites B. L. Whorf on the way in which a given language conditions the sense of time of the people who speak it: "Concepts of 'time' and 'matter' are not given substantially the same form by experience to all men but depend upon the nature of the language or languages through the use of which they have been developed. They do not depend so much upon any one system (e.g., tense, or nouns) within the grammar as upon the ways of analyzing and reporting experience which have become fixed in the language as integrated 'fashions of speaking' and which cut across the typical grammatical classifications" (p. 130).

followers cannot have meant such radical novelty or iconoclasm as is suggested by the metaphors of "death and resurrection," or "rebirth," or such formulations as "the end of the age," or "the end of the law," unless these were all understood in a proleptic sense. Thus Paul's declaration that Christ is "the end of the law" (Rom. 10:4) can hardly be interpreted as "the end of the world," as it sometimes is, unless in a hyperbolic sense to mean that for the individual believer *his* "world" has been changed, or at most that the nature of the creation has been structurally *renewed,* again in a proleptic sense so far as human life is concerned. The "new" race of the Christians could use such expressions for their eschatological awareness and utterance as "new tongues" and "new songs," but the stubborn continuities of human nature are still there, and this is nowhere more evident than in the continuity of human speech habits, whether Jewish or Hellenistic in the church, even when we recognize the large aspects of novelty.

We are confronted here with an absorbing issue. It is no less than that of the stability of human nature, at least in historic times. Surely the factor of language is a significant test. Must not religion, whatever its view of conversion, rebirth, or the spirit, agree with the social scientist that "there must be a permanent foundation in human nature and in human society, or the very names of man and society become meaningless"?[7] A corollary of this stability of human nature is the real continuity of human experience and in this sense of "history." On this view, no instance of cultural iconoclasm, even one so radical as the apocalyptic eschatology of the Gospel, can be an exception, and the continuity of the language of early Christianity with its backgrounds would support this. Will not the theologian, then, agree again with the same social scientist when he observes, "Historical time is a concrete and living reality with an irreversible onward rush. It is the very plasma in which events are immersed, and the field within which they become intelligible. . . . Now this real time is, in essence, a continuum. It is also perpetual change."[8] Ernest Colwell, who cites these passages, indicated their bearing on the study of Christian origins as follows:

> The acceptance of unbroken continuity makes the continuity between Jesus and the Christ of the Church's faith just one instance of a general law of human existence. The acceptance of change that modifies but does not destroy continuity argues against the "either-or" choice which has confused this study many times, e.g., the Jesus of History versus the Christ of Faith, Paul versus the Gospels, the Christ of the Kerygma versus Jesus of Nazareth.[9]

7. Marc Bloch, *The Historian's Craft* (New York, 1953), p. 42.
8. Ibid., pp. 27–28.
9. E. C. Colwell, *Jesus and the Gospel,* (New York, 1963), p. 19.

The idea of continuity or continuum is a notoriously dangerous one, relative as it is to so many exploded views of reality, but the actual continuity of the language of Christianity with its antecedents certainly limits the terms in which we can use absolutes or paradox to describe the new event of the Gospel.

Yet this new event was accompanied by extraordinary novelties in the order of language, and these are a further index of its character. We should not underestimate the degree of sudden change in all that concerns speech which can occasionally be observed. As the analogy of art shows, radically and shockingly new vehicles and motifs can emerge suddenly with the power to establish a new order of reality and a new artistic or rhetorical tradition. In modern letters, the example of the young Rimbaud may be cited: His iconoclasm became the fountainhead of a new poetic and a new surrealist consciousness which has communicated itself powerfully through the generations among poets writing in all languages of the West down to the present day, and has also influenced the other arts.[10]

In the rise of the Gospel, we have a language-event suggested by this analogy, one in which a seismic disturbance overtook existing rhetorics, whether Jewish or Hellenistic. It is therefore of peculiar interest to observe the interplay of tradition and novelty, whether with respect to oral forms like the parable or the rhythmic unit on the lips of Jesus, or with respect to written genres such as the epistle or apocalypse. It is of the first importance that anachronistic categories should be avoided here, especially those of idealism, such as the distinction between form and content, or romantic presuppositions like those suggested by the terms *genius, inspiration,* or *eloquence.* We must also rid ourselves of familiar antitheses like that between spontaneity and art. Thus the novelty in Jesus' use of the traditional genre of the parable (one aspect of which is the fluid variety of this form as he uses it) is related to the eschatological occasion in that in his use of the form the older distinct roles of sage and prophet are transcended.

10. In reaction to the stifling language-reality of his period, Rimbaud immersed himself in a deeper level of consciousness, seeking the "language of the mythic self," his whole effort being, in effect, "an experiment with language." He has been spoken of as one of the "mad who control history," in the sense that those who make language make history. He opened up a new language-reality, a dimension in the modern experience that immediately had authenticity and meaningfulness. His example is a good illustration of what is meant by a *Sprachereignis.* The student of linguistics Alf Sommerfelt cites another case, noting, indeed, the limits within which any such novelty operates: "Among us [i.e., the Norwegians] the poet Wergeland furnishes a fine example of the role of the individual in linguistic evolution. It is well known that he introduced a large number of words and of new forms into Norwegian literature, but it was only those which lent themselves to the exigencies of the movement of *Norvégisation* which were able to establish themselves in the literary language." *Aspects of Language,* p. 47.

Indeed, the novelty of form and import of the parables of the Kingdom reflects the eschatological commitment of the speaker (Fuchs). Furthermore, these features of Jesus' parables by which we recognize in them a relevatory rather than a didactic function corroborate what we would otherwise conclude from the eschatological urgency, that Jesus did not contrive their form to the end of pedagogy or calculated transmission. Without anxiety for the future, or even forethought for the fate or survival of his sayings, Jesus spoke to the immediate occasion. In them the operation of God was opened up, as the finger of God in the exorcisms, and all this belonged to a different world from that of catechesis or learned repetition.

III. SIGNIFICANCE OF THE ORAL MODE

But this issue of convention and novelty in the whole speech-phenomenon of the Gospel bears on larger matters than particular genres and style. We could ask why primitive Christianity confined itself at first so exclusively to the oral mode, and why this mode remained so important even after written texts were introduced. We could ask why anonymity played such a large part in the word of the Gospel for so long a time. We could ask why such ambiguity was possible even as regards the sayings of the Lord—whether they were spoken by Jesus or by the risen Lord in the spirit. We could ask why there is such seeming neglect of the Hebrew tongue and the Hebrew text of the Scriptures in the new Aramaic-speaking movement. This new dynamic speech-world is popular, and not learned; it is secular, and not priestly. We could ask why subsequent translation into the other tongues of the Mediterranean world took place so much as a matter of course. We could ask why no special vocabulary or language of Zion was either espoused or established in the infant church. We could ask why, not only with respect to tongue, but also with respect to semantic and imagery (Christology, soteriology, eschatology), so little resistance was interposed to translation, reformulation, of the new word.

We could ask precisely, and here we take issue with well-known views of Harald Riesenfeld and Birger Gerhardsson, why the transmission of the sayings of Jesus was for long so partial, so unsystematic, and so fortuitous —until a later stage, indeed, when ways of the Jewish or Hellenistic school came into the church. Here we are faced again with the eschatological outlook of Jesus and his disciples and followers. Traditional patterns of teaching and learning were broken by this new occasion. Modalities of language and deportment appropriate to an ongoing society and to settled cultural continuities were inappropriate to the hour of the Kingdom now inaugurated. If the situation had been one in which Jesus had found it suitable to have his disciples repeat and memorize his words, it would also have been one in which he would himself have had a home, a wife, a livelihood. That same eschatological wonder and crisis which explains his saying "Foxes have holes, and birds of the air have nests; but the Son of man has nowhere to lay his head" (Matt. 8:20) also explains the absence of "school" features in the days of his mission.

Also in the days of the post-Easter community, the ethos of the disciples was not that of any other group of Jews. Their situation is to be understood in the light of the saying "What you are to say will be given to you in that hour" (Matt. 10:19). There was no need to memorize and to hoard dominical words and norms; the "word-event" was such that one lived by an ever-new supply. The speech of the Gospel, as Fuchs has remarked, came and went with the freedom of sunshine, wind, and rain.

"Learning" procedures and patterns among other groups of that time can only mislead us, presupposing as they did such different views of time and the divine immediacy. As Riesenfeld says, our judgment here hangs together with our understanding of the Messianic question. On his view, the Messiah formulated a holy Word of the new covenant to be memorized and repeated during a substantial interim. On the other hand, if one sees Jesus as a rabbi, the result is the same, to the degree that a memorized interpretation of the law would follow. But we do not need to adopt either view. The utterance of Jesus had another kind of authority and effect, different from either, associated with his action, rather than his office; an utterance which reproduced itself and renewed itself without prompting, in the very nature of the case.

We have already found ourselves involved in this topic of the oral mode in discussing the sayings of Jesus. From the days of the ancient synagogue down to the late rabbinic colleges, the Jewish Torah was interpreted and taught orally, and only orally, in the scribal and Pharisaic tradition, though some use of private notation was countenanced. In the case of the Sadducees, written halakah of a more formal character was recognized, and of course apocalyptic circles and such an Essenian group as that at Qumran had authoritative sectarian texts alongside the written law and prophets. The oral mode was, then, peculiar to Pharisaic Judaism and the Gospel, but there was a great difference in the grounds for this similar feature, and in the discourse itself. The Pharisees refrained from writing for various reasons listed in an illuminating way by Gerhardsson.[11] They, as a non-priestly group, were conserving a more ancient practice of oral interpreta-

11. *Memory and Manuscript* (Uppsala, 1961), pp. 25, 158. Riesenfeld's position is put forth in his well-known essay, "The Gospel Tradition and Its Beginnings" in his *The Gospel Tradition* (Philadelphia: Fortress Press, 1970), pp. 1–29.

tion of the Torah going back to the third century B.C. Their resistance to writing also represented a reaction to the partial character, as they saw it, of the written tradition of the Sadducees, a reaction stiffened by controversy and confirmed by the development of schools devoted to the study of the oral corpus. They may also have wished to restrict the circle of those who would have access to this body of material.

It would be a mistake to assign only negative reasons for the oral transmission of the tradition of the fathers. The basic motive here, as in the case of Jesus, is immediacy, though not as in his case in the context of an imminent eschatological urgency. The immediacy which conditioned the oral Torah was that of the *present,* distinguished from the past of Sinai. The Torah must be accomplished here and now in personal responsibility, and the urgency of obedience in the present imposes oral formulation, for only so is the instruction of God lively in the present.

> Against the Sadducees, [the Pharisees] were so bold as to erect the oral tradition to the rank of Torah—calling it the unwritten Torah—and to use it as contemporary and living divine instruction that could serve as guide and interpreter to the written text of the Pentateuch. . . . Thus the Torah became inexhaustible, plastic and not static . . . the interpretation of the Torah became open, in accordance with the remark of a late rabbi: "Whatever an acute disciple shall hereafter teach in the presence of his Rabbi has already been said to Moses on Sinai" (cited by T. Herford, *The Pharisees* [1924], p. 85).[12]

There was then no eschatological factor in the oral method of the Pharisees, though it did reflect a sense of the living word. Yet their instruction and legislation reckoned with ongoing time. Though this sense of unbroken continuities and a future did not, in their case, reflect itself in the social convention of writing, it did adopt the related art of an oral rhetoric calculated for survival: an elaborate use of mnemonic devices facilitating a total transmission.

Such prudential considerations seem to have been absent in the case of Jesus. We should not, indeed, think in a romantic way about the spontaneity of his utterance, but neither should we be misled by the later stage of transmissions or by such an evangelist as Matthew in identifying him as a second Moses or a catechist. The immediacy and directness of Jesus' call and warnings and celebration of the time of salvation—these imposed extempore oral address. This lack of concern for the survival of his words corresponds, as we have suggested, to his detachment from the usual cultural bonds of ongoing society, and his demeanor in both respects has the

12. P. Ricoeur, *Finitude et culpabilité* II, *La symbolique du mal,* (Paris, 1960), pp. 122–23.

force of an acted parable. The significance of this mode of life and of speech is further indicated by his charge to the disciples, as they went out two by two, not to instruct but to utter a cry, to heal, and to exorcize. If purse and wallet were forbidden them, we may be sure that no equipment for writing was to be found in their girdles.

We would say, then, that with his sense of the eschatological crisis, Jesus took no thought for the precariousness of oral speech. One argument that is formulated against this view invokes the poetic structure of his sayings. But here we meet a clear example of inappropriate categories. It is true that for our modern, as for classical rhetoric, formal artistry and creative spontaneity are mutually exclusive. Applying these distinctions between the sophisticated and the naive to early Christian material, scholars conclude that the strophic aspect of the sayings of Jesus indicates a calculated "artistic" procedure designed to render his teaching easy to memorize. Thus Matthew Black writes: "Jesus did not commit anything to writing, but by His use of poetic form and language, He insured that His sayings would not be forgotten. The impression they make in Aramaic is of carefully premeditated and studied deliverances."[13] It is an analogous presupposition which leads some to identify 1 Corinthians 13 as a kind of poem of Paul's which he chose to insert at this point. Ernst Käsemann has had occasion to protest against such modernization in connection with formulas of the early Christian prophets. It is argued that because the formulas have rhythmic structure, they are too artistic to be assignable to visionary apocalyptic oracles. But Käsemann rightly observes that "primitive Christianity, as is shown both in its hymns and in the 'He who overcomes' sayings in Revelation, did in fact ascribe to the Spirit this precise capacity of combining concentrated content and artistic form."[14] Formal sophistication is perfectly compatible with prophetic and, indeed, extempore utterance. Likewise, with respect to Jesus' sayings about Jonah and the Queen of the South, the same writer observes, "Only a false conception of inspiration as resulting in an uncontrolled outburst of feeling can enter this [such poetic form] in evidence against the presence of prophecy here."[15]

The oral and face-to-face address of Jesus to his generation is of a piece with his understanding of his role, that of mediator of God's final controversy with his people. God's dealing with Israel in the past had often taken

13. *An Aramaic Approach to the Gospels*, (2d ed., 1957), p. 142.

14. "The Beginnings of Christian Theology," in *New Testament Questions of Today*, tr. W. J. Montague (Philadelphia: Fortress Press, 1969), p. 96.

15. Ibid., p. 95.

on the character of a judicial hearing in which the parties confront each other in direct indictment and reply. So here Jesus' summons, plea, warnings, and judgment represent the appropriate forensic gestures in the situation. No trial can take place by correspondence. The situation of immediate, living dialogue is also suggested in Jesus' instructions to his disciples, which may be taken as a paradigm of his entire mission:

> Whatever house you enter, first say, "Peace be to this house!" And if a son of peace is there your peace shall rest upon him; but if not it shall return to you. (Luke 10:6).

The language of the Gospel as a whole continued to have this personal, fateful character of dialogue, and inevitably transcended the speech forms of its environment. Even the later written texts of the New Testament are shaped by this factor. The living and acting word of God, which lays all things bare, accounts for the large place in the New Testament writings of such oral features as direct discourse, dialogue forms, and the use of the second person.

The eschatological consciousness which determines the oral character of Jesus' speech also influences details of that speech such as style and genre. We have noted the novelty of his use of the parable. We have noted the secular ethos of his sayings: as one speaking in the hour of the Kingdom, the culture-models of wisdom, law, and even prophecy are transformed when he uses them. The eschatological determination of his way of speaking appears, of course, in its thematic content—its concern with judgment and the new age, with Satan, demons, and angels, with corresponding rewards and penalties. But this also appears in the prominence of formulas of blessing and woe; of adversative couplets of losing and finding, first and last, least and greatest; of dual formulas reflecting the coincidence of the old age and the new, though based on the older temporal polarity of the two;[16] of paradox and hyperbole; and not least in the brevity of his speech and speech forms, constituting a radical purification of human language. All of this contrasts with the forms, diction, styles, vocabulary, and imagery found in the rhetorics of Qumran, the apocalyptic circles, and the synagogue. In this *Sprachwesen* of the Gospel, in the case first of Jesus himself and then in the Jesus-tradition of the Palestinian-Aramaic church, we can recognize a new liberty of utterance and a radical fulfillment of earlier modalities of utterance and communication. And it was determined by the eruption of the Kingdom and the underlying revolution in the sense of time and all other realities.

16. Cf. Robinson, *Kerygma,* chap. 6.

6

The Symbolic Realism of Jesus' Language

The flesh does not inherit, but is inherited; as also the
Lord declares, "Blessed are the meek, for they shall possess the earth by inheritance," as if in the kingdom, the
earth, from whence exists the substance of our flesh, is to
be possessed by inheritance.

Ireneaus, *Adv. Haer*, v, ix.4.

I. DECODING HIEROGLYPHS

Ancient eschatological texts are, as literary remains, undecoded hieroglyphs
and enigmas unless we are able to recreate the world of experience of
which they are only ambiguous tokens. Modern study of biblical eschatology is constantly confronted with problems as to the proper interpretation
of the cosmic and transcendental language. Depending on the content, such
questions arise as the following: Did the writer mean his words to be
taken literally—including the references to immediate fulfillment? Are they
to be read as "Oriental poetry," or as "poetic heightening," or as an
"accommodation to language"? Are we to take the figurative discourse as
a "clothing" of otherwise incommunicable revelation or vision? Is the cosmic language supposed to refer to "spiritual"—that is, supermundane realities—or to such realities seen as paralleling earthly phenomena; or is it
rather an imaginative version of the earthly phenomena themselves? At
what points are we to recognize more or less transparent historization of
older myth and symbol? Does the eschatological imagery of Deutero-
Isaiah represent merely a poetic idealization of a mundane New Age, while
that of the late apocalypses denotes the absolute end of all created existence?[1] Does this later dualistic eschatology signify, in fact, the end of the

1. Cf. J. A. T. Robinson, *Jesus and His Coming* (New York, 1957), pp. 94–97.

133

world and a sheerly miraculous future state, or does it teach by hyperbole the transformation of the world?[2]

Our purpose here is to explore these matters in the writings. Our attention will be given chiefly to the problem of the right approach to the imagery in question. Modern students of symbolism and semantic outside the biblical field have much to contribute, as do students of Utopian movements in their relation to social crises. Basic to this paper are two considerations which, we believe, will do much to clarify the problem before us.

The first consideration has to do with the imagery itself and its genesis. We urge that, especially for our greater texts, full recognition be given to the operation of the "mythical mentality," in all its creative and quasi-magical power. In the second place, we urge recognition of the sociological setting of the eschatology. The very impulse to such dualistic interpretation of the world-process rises out of a radical culture-crisis in Judaism, but, in addition, the cosmic-eschatological language in many respects exhibits its relation to earthly situations, events, and outcomes.

We believe that if these two considerations are given their weight, many issues in contemporary study will be illuminated, such as the radical immediacy of Jesus' expectation of the Kingdom; the relation of his ministry to the political and social actualities of Jewish life; the significance of the delay of the consummation; Paul's mythical realism and his view of the angelic powers; and the secondary appropriation in the Gospels and the later New Testament writings of apocalyptic motifs.

II. MYTH AND THE TRANSFIGURATION OF THE WORLD

Religion commonly posits various forms of dualism and polarity in its portrayal of man's existence. These dualisms relate first of all to his sense of dependence on the source of his being, but inevitably appear also in the portrayal of his ultimate destiny. The terms in which he sets forth the invisible realities of either theology or eschatology are evidently drawn from his mundane experience in various degrees of depth and self-under-

---

2. Note the contortions of R. H. Charles in dealing with the various characterizations of the New Age in Isa. 51:6; 60:19; 65:17, and 66:22. Are they to be taken literally or poetically? The first passage, he says, expresses its view of the end of the old heaven and earth "not as an eschatological doctrine but poetically." The last two, on the other hand, are "obviously" to be taken literally. *A Critical History of the Doctrine of the Future Life* (1913), p. 129. Cf. also W. O. E. Oesterley, *The Book of Enoch* (London: S.P.C.K., 1925), pp. ix–x, for a characteristic but questionable view of apocalyptic symbol.

standing. In the case of Jewish-Christian eschatology, we rightly emphasize the peculiar social-historical concreteness and moral life-experience which underlie the eschatological hope.

While scholars have, of course, recognized that particular prophecies and apocalypses arose out of particular crises and situations, we are convinced that the full significance of this matter is not grasped. Biblical theologians tend to create too great a disjunction between the transcendental imagery and the historical process. They see the reality conveyed as belonging to the sphere of sheer idealization and fantasy. Or they allow a metaphysical or theological dualism to obscure the concrete meaning of the texts. Too often they fail to enter into the late Jewish and early Christian mythical frame of mind.

Students of eschatology have given comparatively little attention to the semantic question proper in dealing with their texts. If one looks into such works as those of Volz, Charles, Bousset, and Althaus, one finds no prolegomenon or section on the hermeneutic and semantic problem set by the mythopoetic character of the material. It is not enough to trace the antecedents of the material, to identify its cult relationships and formal features or its overt historical allusions, or to make an inventory of the religious ideas found in it.

One basic issue arises in connection with the definition of eschatology. Its essential reference is commonly thought of as being to nonhuman and nontemporal reality. Thus van der Leeuw describes it as referring to "events at the margin of the world before it was world, and after it has ceased to be world."[3] He relates it to its counterpart in the *creatio ex nihilo*. He contrasts eschatological thinking with cyclical thinking. Primitive man is not historically conscious; he had no eschatology; the world is renewed for him in annual rites, and the more elaborate cyclical conceptions share his outlook. Eschatological conceptions dawn "only after man has made a considerable advance in his painful awakening to consciousness, and the suffering of human existence has set itself a term either in a supreme terror or in an infinite bliss. The stupendous idea of an end of time is an attempt to negate the eternal stasis, to break the circle." Thus van der Leeuw sees "a great cleavage in the self-consciousness of mankind. On the one side, time takes a cyclical course, on the other it has a beginning before which there was nothing and an end with which it stops."[4] The imminent eschatology of the New Testament is to be seen in this light.

---

3. "Primordial Time and Final Time," in *Man and Time,* Papers from the Eranos Yearbooks, no. 3 (New York, 1957), p. 337.

4. Ibid., p. 338.

When time stops, the "future" can only be described in terms of impossible fictions, *adunata*.

Now it is of interest here that the very possibility of eschatology is seen in terms of man's awakening to genuine historical consciousness. Van der Leeuw also sees the Christian period, the *Christiana tempora,* as arising out of the Christ-drama in history. What is to be rejected here, however, is the radical nontemporal view of eschatology. To speak in our terms of "the end" of the world or of the "events at the margin of the world" is not to think biblically. We must indeed recognize the final element of freedom in God involved in eschatology as in creation, but the impulse in Jewish-Christian eschatology to "negate the eternal stasis, to break the circle" of human suffering calls for the redemption of time, and not its end. The eschatological myth dramatizes the transfiguration of the world, and is not a mere poetry of an unthinkable, atemporal state.[5]

It is significant that the emergence of highly dualistic views of the end-time runs parallel with a more and more explicit doctrine of the *creatio ex nihilo,* as well as with emphasis on miracle.[6] All three are motivated by the desire to express the transcendence of God and the absolute dependence of the universe upon him. The explicit doctrine of the end of the world (2 Macc., 2 En., and Tatian), like the explicit doctrine of the *creatio ex nihilo* (Hermas), arises out of apologetic or speculative motives. The New Testament nowhere explicitly states that God made the world out of nothing; its writers point that way, just as they point in various ways to an acosmic future. A pedagogical and apologetic motive impels them

---

5. Karl Mannheim's characterization of the radical ecstatic outlook of Chiliasm among the Anabaptists suggests the dissociation of the eschatological "world" from that of history. "The only true, perhaps the only direct identifying characteristic of Chiliast experience, is absolute presentness. We always occupy some here and now in the spatial and temporal stage but, from the point of view of Chiliast experience, the position that we occupy is only incidenta!. For the real Chiliast, the present becomes the breach through which what was previously inward bursts out suddenly, takes hold of the outer world and transforms it." Mannheim then speaks of the "tense expectation" of the Chiliast. "He is always on his toes awaiting the propitious moment and thus there is no inner articulation of time for him. He is not actually concerned with the millenium that is to come." *Ideology and Utopia* (New York: 1936), pp. 215–16. This description well suggests the ecstatic character of early Christian eschatology in its primary form. But the latter was conceived in a Jewish historical-teleological background, while the Chiliasm in question was heavily colored by a specifically mystical strain. The atemporal eschaton defined by van der Leeuw fits this type of Chiliasm and some expressions of deviant Jewish and early Christian eschatology better than it does the primary eschatology of Jesus and the New Testament.

6. On the correlation of miracle, *creatio ex nihilo,* and eschatology, see R. M. Grant, *Miracle and Natural Law* (1952), chaps. 10–11.

toward a highly dualistic eschatology, but the characteristic imagery every-where suggests a renewed or fulfilled creation, not an acosmic state.[7]

The eschatological imagery of early Christianity has a long prehistory in Judaism, Israel, and the ancient Near East. The material, in all its multitudinous forms, bears the marks of centuries and epochs of man's social history and of the "political" patterns of that history,[8] as well as of his relation to what we call nature. The vehicles employed to portray the future are both social and cosmic. But social and cosmic elements are interfused, as we may well understand in the light of the way that at least these ancients understood existence.[9] In any case, the eschatological im-agery with which we are concerned was redolent of man's long cultural past and drew its meaning from that heritage. The future hope could not be for them in any sense a *novum;* it could not represent a truncation with the past, a discontinuity.

There is indeed one further feature of the prehistory of our material. It reflected not only successive layers of the older social and cosmic envi-ronments, but also recognition of an extrasocial and extracosmic operation of God associated with the idea of his freedom and purpose. This dynamic teleological motif was, however, discovered in the social experience and vicissitudes of Israel and was inextricably inwrought in its moral-historical

---

7. Paul Althaus well indicates not only that the glory of God would be diminished if in the Kingdom there were radical devaluations of the personal life of the creature, but also that eternal life requires the element of "world." It is not only a matter of *"Innerlichkeit."* The creation is not just a preliminary means or scaffolding, for God rejoices in his works, and these endure. *Die letzten Dinge* (1956), pp. 321–22, 343–44. The present and coming eons in the New Testament "are not related as earth and heaven, as *Diesseits* and *Jenseits,* but the new eon breaks into our world, into this history, and transforms it" (p. 361).

8. "The Israelite kingship, the sociological structure of the Israelites, their religious life, condensed in holy scriptures, their worship and rites, all these are elements in a long process which—from the point of view of the New Testament—can be charac-terized as a preparation or prefiguration, a time of forming and molding of the terms and metaphors and thoughts, the existence of which was a necessary condition for the proclamation of the gospel by Jesus and for the belief of the church from its very beginning." H. Riesenfeld, "The Mythological Background of Christology," in *The Background of the New Testament and Its Eschatology,* ed. W. D. Davies and D. Daube (1956), p. 86 (also in Riesenfeld's *The Gospel Tradition* [Philadelphia: Fortress Press, 1970], pp. 37–38).

9. "Just as Hebrew psychology ascribed psychical qualities to the physical organs and made the body an essential part of human personality, so Hebrew philosophy (if the term may be allowed) ascribed metaphysical significance to events in the external world, and made these (as symbols) parts of a larger whole of reality. . . . We start from an implicit dualism between the material and the spiritual. . . . Their antithesis was not that of mind and matter, but of God and man." H. W. Robinson, "Prophetic Symbolism," in *Old Testament Essays: Papers Read before the Society for Old Testament Study* (1927), pp. 11–12.

consciousness. Even the apocalyptic stage of Jewish eschatology and the accompanying tendency toward individualism could not dissolve the relation between the future redemption and the concrete social history of the past, although sometimes, as in the case of the Hellenistic Jewish eschatology, much of the rich corporate substance of the ancient legacy was forfeited. This loss of corporate and cosmic concern in the late Jewish eschatology, as in some early Christian eschatology, wherever it occurred, represented a radical impoverishment of the tradition and the faith. The early Christian dualistic eschatology in the main continued or repossessed the Jewish tradition in its social-cosmic realism, at the same time that it recognized the creative operation of God inseparably related to it. That new thing which God was doing, had done, would do was not a discontinuous *novum*; it could only be understood in terms of the imagery of the past and of the life experience from which that imagery was drawn.

For the purposes of our discussion, we may note four aspects of our topic with which we may assume general agreement. Our argument carries beyond these matters generally recognized, but they are relevant to it. 1) At least some apocalyptic writings were occasioned by a very specific historical crisis of Israel or of the church. This is no doubt a truism as regards writings like Daniel, the Fourth Book of Ezra, and Revelation. But the occasion for such writings in their real vitality is much more than a mere "political" conjuncture, and many such texts relate to cultural, rather than to political situations. 2) Traditional eschatological symbol is, as we say, "historicized" and rehistoricized in innumerable instances. This, again, is familiar, and we shall not need to document it. 3) The cult and festival focus or life situation of much eschatological tradition and expression is to be recognized.[10] If we appreciate that cult-eschatology is a genuinely *popular* phenomenon in Christianity and Judaism (compare Bo Reicke, *Diakonie, Festfreude und Zelos*)[11] we shall not be disposed to read it in an abstractly theological way. 4) The portrayal of the New Age, and indeed of heavenly realities in general, is in terms of mundane experience. Here the fact that the ancient writers are confined to earthly imagery to describe transcendental felicity does not disqualify that mode of representation as meaningless or fictional.

Agreement in such matters, however, falls far short, in our opinion, of an adequate view of the mundane reference and relevance of our eschatology. Misunderstanding, as we see it, arises at a rhetorical and semantic

---

10. For examples: H. Riesenfeld, *The Gospel Tradition*, pp. 81–95; O. Cullmann, *Early Christian Worship* (London: SCM, 1953), pp. 87–88, 91–92.
11. Uppsala, 1951.

level in dealing with the texts, at a theological level in dealing with the world views and dualisms involved, and at an historical level in dealing with the life situations which reflect themselves in the transcendental vehicles.

III. THE MYTHOPOESIS OF JESUS

The first two points can be best taken up together. If we are "in contact with the ancient eschatological way of feeling" (Rudolf Otto), we are at the same time prepared to recognize the true character of the dualism which it inspires or borrows. The ecstatic or visionary state does not postulate cosmological or metaphysical dualism in any rational or secular sense. What is expressed is not a mere matter of feeling. It represents genuine cognition and affirmation, but what is stated is mythopoetic, and not easily reducible to our categories of world view and time view. The transcendental imagery does not lend itself to our spacial distinctions between mundane and supermundane, nor even to our temporal distinctions of present and future or to our periodizations.

We are speaking now not of derivative apocalyptic expressions, but of those of figures like the Baptist, Jesus, and Paul, in whom we can recognize original and fresh mythological vision. Here we have that kind of primal image-making power associated by students of early cultures with epiphany phenomena, the genesis of myth and ritual, and the naming of things. Writers like Cassirer, Tillich, and van der Leeuw[12] have dealt with this kind of world-shaping imagination, often in dependence upon the anthropologist.[13] Contemporary literary critics (such as T. S. Eliot, Herbert Read, Allen Tate, Philip Wheelwright, Jacques Maritain, etc.), discussing the language of poetry, have also illuminated these dimensions of pre-logical conception and its rhetoric.

Significant features of the mythical mentality are: the intensity of the experience, carrying with it unshakeable belief; the sense of the givenness of the revelation; the social context of the epiphany; the synthesizing of cosmic-social reality; and the merging of seer with group and of subject with object. In such ecstatic apprehension, ordinary distinctions of the categories are transcended: time, space, and causation. The resulting word or oracle, in its symbolic condensation, does not represent, or tell about,

12. For van der Leeuw, see "Primordial Time," pp. 350–55.

13. In the field of early Greek religion, the work of W. F. Otto is particularly illuminating, especially *Dionysos, Mythos und Kultur* (Frankfurt-am-Main: Klostermann, 1933). On the Semitic side: ed., H. Frankfort, *Before Philosophy* (Baltimore: Penguin, 1949) and E. R. Goodenough, *Jewish Symbols*, vol. 4 (1954), chap. 2.

or imitate what is given, but is identified with it: "the word must be the thing it represents, otherwise it is (only) a symbol" (Wallace Stevens); it is "reality *lived* . . . , a statement of primeval reality" (Malinowski); it has "arcane and potent force" (Pettazzoni).

Placing the eschatology of Jesus in this context, we can recognize that his message crystallized profound insight into the reality of his own social situation and gave to it a mythological statement. The power of the spell cast as always by such momentous vision or epiphany inevitably created a radical cleavage with existing patterns, apart from those which it took up into itself and transformed. Mythical thinking in its pure state is an "enclosed realm." Thus we can understand the dichotomies in early Christian world view. But they are not dichotomies between eschatology and history in the usual sense: the eschatology includes the history. It is not a dualism between transcendent and mundane realities: the transcendent here include the mundane. Therefore Jesus' so-called dualistic representation of his time and the future was, in fact, a vision of history as a whole, a transfiguration of the given world, and not an escape from or a denial of it.[14] Similarly, Paul's eschatology was a vision of history (no doubt carrying with it a rejection of a moribund aspect of history) in which, indeed, here and there what we would call mundane elements show through transparently.

When we speak thus of the ecstatic and visionary character of the eschatological outlook, we are not identifying ourselves with a romantic, idealistic, or aesthetic view. Even the charismatic conception of Rudolf Otto calls for caution. Otto rightly drew attention to the dynamic dimension of early Christian life and thought, but he was much taken up with supernormal experience and spiritism.

The world-representation of Jesus was not spiritistic; in his case the visionary content is conditioned by the biblical realism of his background. Paul knew how to disparage spiritistic endowment. Spiritism indeed lends itself to a systematic and world-disparaging dualism. The eschatological vision of Jesus and Paul was prophetic and evangelical, and therefore not

14. What Karl Mannheim says about Utopian symbolism and the tension between the new order proclaimed and the old order devalued needs to be corrected in our context by the differentia of early Christian faith. It is nevertheless illuminating. "The first stirrings of what is new . . . are in fact oriented towards the existing order and . . . the existing order is itself rooted in the alignment and tension of the forces of social life. . . . What is new in the achievement of the personally unique 'charismatic' individual can only then be utilized for the collective life when, from the very beginning, it is in contact with some important current problem, and when from the start its meanings are rooted genetically in collective purposes." *Ideology and Utopia*, pp. 206–7.

dualistic; it was concerned with the course of the world under God's providence. In the case of Paul, this actually emerges into a kind of historization, especially in Romans, chapters 9 through 11,[15] and in his interpretation of the cosmic struggle.

Thus the most significant eschatology of early Christianity is to be understood in terms of symbolic realism.[16] The interpretation of the figurative material in the Bible has too often been carried out under the sway of that idealist aesthetic which has so long dominated humanistic and literary studies. This approach makes much of rhetoric and eloquence as the language of the soul or the external clothing of thought. It sets the realm of imagination over against life. It distinguishes wrongly between form and content. It is not surprising that eschatology is heavily discounted by this kind of prepossession. But its symbols are not merely rhetoric and decoration. They are real media of power and life. Metaphor and trope constitute essential vehicles of the Gospel itself. They not only dramatize it, but they participate in it; they define world view and history-view at the same time that they renew our world and our history. They give order to chaos and identify us with that which creates order. Primary myth is always both aesthetic and cognitive, but it is also a vehicle of life itself.[17]

IV. FROM EPIPHANY TO ART

We have been speaking of the eschatological mood in its primal power and visionary character. We do need, however, to take account of the fact that, as with all myth, this intensity tended to give way to more realistic states of mind. When this happened, the imagery born in an incandescent state tended to harden. Less inspired individuals, groups, and sects then used the originally creative legacy in new ways, and began to relate it to more conventional categories of time, space, and causation. Here we find that

15. N. H. Dahl, reviewing Rudolf Bultmann's *Theologie des Neuen Testaments,* argues with special reference to Romans 9 through 11 that even for Paul the Christ-event cannot be understood as the end of the "world." *Theologische Rundschau* 22 (1954):21–49.

16. Austin Farrer speaks well of these matters. "Symbol endeavours, as it were, to *be* that of which it speaks. . . . There is a current and exceedingly stupid doctrine that symbol evokes emotion, and exact prose states reality. . . . Nothing could be further from the truth: exact prose abstracts from reality, symbol presents it." *A Rebirth of Images* (London: Dacre Press, 1949), pp. 19–20.

17. Ezra Pound's characterization of the poetic image is suggestive: "It is a vortex or cluster of fused ideas and is endowed with energy . . . , it presents an intellectual and emotional complex in an instant of time . . . , gives that sense of sudden liberation; that sense of freedom from time and space limits; that sense of sudden growth, which we experience in the presence of the greatest art." Cited by E. Miner, "Pound, Haiku and the Image," *Hudson Review* 9:4 (1956–57):576.

manifold linking of the mythical dimension with particular aspects of history and cosmology which we speak of as historization, calculation of the times, speculation and curiosity, rationalization, and so forth—that is, various degrees of schematization. We are familiar with such conventionalizing of the mythical perspective in our Jewish apocalypses and in the Christian literature. Some of this represents an evacuation of the substance of the eschatological vision. But we should not confuse this with the continuation of vital myth-making prophecy adapted to ongoing historical circumstances.

We may take, for example, what happened to Jesus' expectation of the Kingdom. He saw this in visionary immediacy: it is the very character of such ecstatic mythical intensity to dissolve and transcend time categories. His outlook could not have had a place in it for an interim. Yet the legacy of the older universalist hope, with its anticipation, for example, of the conversion of the Gentiles, would have been implicit and, as it were, hidden in his instantaneous teleological affirmation. We would also conclude that Jesus expected no historical church. Yet the transcendent Kingdom which he acclaimed was not therefore nonhistorical or acosmic. These categories are not suitable. Just as we should not misread the mythological symbol in modernizing idealist categories, so we should not do so in metaphysical categories.[18]

The fact is that the primitive community in Jerusalem, as well as the church as we know it in Paul's letters, not only saw itself in mythological terms, but actually lived and worshipped "in history" in the spell and power of the mythical mentality. This meant that it saw itself as belonging to quite a different order of reality from that of its Jewish or pagan environment.[19] In this respect the church actually did have a character anticipated in Jesus' transcendental eschatology. It is therefore understandable that it assigned to Jesus sayings about the church in its empirical, institutional aspect. Here, as in other respects, the instantaneous epiphanic outlook of Jesus could take on a phased articulation in contact with actual circumstances. Similarly, Jesus' own expectation of immediate exaltation at his death—and the initial view of his resurrection as an aspect of the

18. The remarks of Frank M. Cross, Jr., on the Essene apocalyptic exegesis are relevant: "Some attempt has been made on the part of scholars to distinguish between purely historical commentary and purely eschatological, or between commentaries dealing primarily with external history and those dealing primarily with internal history. Such distinctions involve categories foreign to the apocalyptic mind, and can be applied to Essene materials only by forcing and distortion." *The Ancient Library of Qumran and Modern Biblical Studies* (New York: Doubleday, 1958), p. 85, n. 9.

19. Since the pagan world also understood itself in its own mythical way, the issue was that of two orders of myth, rather than of a contrast of myth and history.

consummation itself—could later take on various phases in the reflective elaboration of the church as it distinguished between resurrection, ascension, gift of the Spirit, submission of the angelic powers, and Parousia. In the one case, that of Jesus, we have the ecstatic apprehension of immediate vindication. In the other case, that of the church, with much variety, we have schematizations which in their various detail are still sustained by the prophetic-mythical impulse, that is, by the Spirit.

When the dynamic character of early Christian eschatology is rightly grasped, the problem of the delay of the end or Parousia is better understood. Such delay would not be a significant consideration so long as the mythical-eschatological intensity and dimension were transmitted. The imminent expectation had an ecstatic character which would repel such rationalization. And in fact this depth of experience and of interpretation of "history" continued in the church, even though it took on new expression, including, as Hans Conzelmann says, "old apocalyptic conceptions." We cannot, however, agree with Conzelmann when he writes: "It is only the ideas concerning what is hoped for, not the hope itself, that can be transmitted."[20] What is transmitted through the decades, we would rather say, is the Gospel itself, with its eschatological consciousness and passion, and its teleological demand. This takes on different cultural categories and time concepts, but as long as it is mythically powerful it dominates the delay and is not dominated by it.

What we have to reckon with is not the delay of the Parousia, but relaxation of the initial eschatological tension, the cooling of the original incandescence. This could happen in either of two ways. It could reflect an impoverishment of the Gospel itself. In such cases the problem of the delay would emerge, since in such circles the mythology would become empty and therefore subject to rationalization. Professor Bo Reicke has given rich illustration of this kind of problematic in his *Diakonie, Festfreude und Zelos* (see n. 11). Here the eschatology is secularized and occasions either impatience and disenchantment or turns to hedonism, *Schwärmerei,* and religiopolitical agitation. We would judge that the concern for the delay evidenced in the Gospel of Matthew, for example, is directed to such phenomena among those whose love is growing cold, but is not a primary problem for the author himself. The *ecclesia* in Matthew has, all in all, an eschatological, not an institutional character, as Günther Bornkamm has pointed out, drawing the contrast with the highly institu-

---

20. *The Theology of St. Luke,* tr. G. Buswell (New York: Harper & Row, 1960), p. 97.

tionalized Qumran community.[21] For this reason the problem of delay is not central in Matthew. The prominent apocalyptic features are to be understood as serving homiletical and catechetical purposes.

Or again, the eschatological tension would become relaxed in normal course with the passage of time as the continuing novelty and ardor of the Gospel found expression in new categories. We find examples in Hebrews, Ephesians, and the Gospel of John. In this case the issue of the delay would indeed emerge, since the imminent expectation would have become a somewhat formalized survival, but here the issue would be of marginal importance over against the new vehicles of faith. It was not the problem of the delay which occasioned the new forms of soteriology, ecclesiology, and so forth. Rather the new sociological and cultural setting of the church occasioned its new self-interpretation in creative fashion.

In Luke-Acts we have a kind of historization of the course of salvation and of eschatology, though not of the end-event itself, which is objectified and removed to a further future.[22] The work of this author thus forfeits a great deal of the primal dynamic of the earlier vision, but compensates for the loss in its own way. We are to see his work as a schematization and humanization of what was actually implicit in the earlier mythical view of Jesus and the first community.[23]

The breaking up of the earlier apocalyptic immediacy into temporal stages and successions, and the accompanying importation of cosmological and gnostic motifs, is not in itself to be viewed as loss or infidelity in the church. The so-called Hellenization of early Christianity is an example of

21. "Enderwartung und Kirche im Matthäusevangelium," in W. D. Davies and D. Daube, eds., *The Background of the New Testament and Its Eschatology* (Cambridge: Cambridge University Press, 1956), pp. 247–59. Note also the mythical-sacral world in which the Pauline churches lived, as notably brought out in E. Käsemann's article, "Sätze heiligen Rechtes im Neuen Testament," N.T.S. (1955): 248–60. ("Sentences of Holy Law in the New Testament" in *New Testament Questions of Today*, tr. W. J. Montague [Philadelphia: Fortress Press, 1969], pp. 23–65).

22. H. Conzelmann, *The Theology of St. Luke*, pt. 2. G. Harder, in *Theologia Viatorum* 4 (1952):100–101. Professor Henry Cadbury rightly stresses the objective reality assigned by Luke to the eschatological hopes and events. "The resurrection, the Spirit, and the *parousia* were not for him to be transferred to events of mere imagination, or to be regarded as poetical expressions but to be understood quite literally." In W. D. Davies and D. Daube, eds., *The Background of the New Testament and Its Eschatology*, p. 303. Cf. Conzelmann: "There is no unrestrained symbolism in Luke" (*Theology of St. Luke*, p. 34). No New Testament eschatology was vaguely symbolic in the "poetic" sense, but in Luke we recognize an objectifying or hardening tendency which forfeits the original connotative power and mystery. Myth and epiphany become art.

23. E. Fuchs well cautions against overemphasis on the delay factor in our reading of Luke–Acts, *Hermeneutik*, 1st ed. (Bad Cannstatt: R. Müllerschön Verlag, 1954), p. 165; see context, p. 163.

the familiar transition from mythos to logos, or epiphany to art. The initial eschatological impulse was in process of assimilating and ordering the current elements and traditions of the wider world. As Johannes Quispel says, with reference to the patristic period, "Ironically enough, it would seem to have been through eschatology that elements having their origin in the mysteries, in philosophy, and in the Gnoses of antiquity became integrated into Christianity."[24]

V. THE EARTHLY REALISM OF JESUS

We have tried to show that the original impulse of Christian eschatology was not dualistic in our modern sense. We can illustrate in the case of Jesus himself. J. A. T. Robinson, in his book *Jesus and His Coming,* speaks of Jesus' awareness of the historical events of his time, and of the transcendental terms in which he necessarily characterized these and their outcomes. "To use such language," Robinson writes, "was not in itself to abandon historical expectation for something purely mythological."[25] This is surely correct. Robinson relates this emphasis, however, to his view that the eschatological symbol of Jesus in its future aspect was only a sign for the "great Henceforth" and that its chief significance was to clarify the importance of his present mission and person. The subsequent apocalyptic schematization carried out by the church thus represented a secondary concern with the time problem and the future goal or Parousia.

We would prefer to think that the church was merely articulating a genuine teleological element in Jesus' thought, and that he announced a total redemption of man and the world, and not only a "great Henceforth." His frame of reference was theocentric and cosmic-historical, rather than "messianic." It is worth noting that emphasis on realized or inaugurated eschatology, at the expense of futurist eschatology, in Jesus is often linked on the part of the modern interpreter with an insistence in one form or other on Jesus' messianic consciousness.

No doubt in our Gospels the relation of the historical Jesus to his time and place is deeply obscured beneath depth on depth of intervening overlays. We only dimly descry the actualities of his days, like those who behold the ocean floor through the refracting waters. The obscurity is due not only to omissions and distortions of the tradition, but also to the fact that Jesus himself interpreted the situation of his time in what are to us non-realistic ways.

24. "Time and History in Patristic Christianity," in *Man and Time,* Papers from the Eranos Yearbooks, no. 3 (New York, 1957), p. 89.
25. P. 98.

Nevertheless his career and message were realistically related to the occasion. This judgment is not to be taken in a superficial sense. If we reject views that Jesus' outlook was "purely religious" or "purely spiritual," or exclusively "eschatological," we must also reject views associated with Eisler, Simkhovich, and others that Jesus was motivated largely by political or economic factors of his day. There is a more significant way to understand his historical awareness and contemporaneity. As Karl Barth has said, "The World became Jewish flesh."[26] We know that the eschatological consciousness and tension of the Qumran community was directed to an historical situation or situations, to events, parties, and individuals. All these were read in such mythological terms that we have difficulty in making the appropriate identifications. Yet, as Frank M. Cross, Jr., has written, "The Essene literature enables us to discover the concrete Jewish setting in which an apocalyptic understanding of history was living and integral to community existence."[27]

Jesus' transcendental interpretation of his time had an analogous relation to real situations, but of a deeper kind. Such features as the political dilemma, poverty, and Jewish social authority are in view and sometimes come to the fore, but these are absorbed in the deeper crisis. The eruption and appeal of apocalyptic vision of this kind is occasioned by radical cultural disorder, by the loss of meaning of inherited symbols and rites,[28] and such was the Jewish situation in the time of Jesus, as it was in another sense for large groups in the Hellenistic world.

We are confronted again with the real depth of mythological perception. What Ernst Fuchs says about this in his *Hermeneutik* is pertinent. He recognizes its epiphanic character and elemental dynamics.[29] He also urges the historical relatedness of the early Christian myth and eschatology as against existentialist views.[30] This kind of world-shaping myth sets itself

26. *Kirchliche Dogmatik,* IV/1 (Zürich, 1953), p. 181.

27. *Ancient Library,* p. 151.

28. In the words of G. Bornkamm, Jesus did his work "in a world which had lost the present, because it lived between the past and the future, between traditions and promises or threats." *Jesus of Nazareth* (New York: Harper & Row, 1960), p. 58. Cf. G. von Rad on conditions at the time of the rise of the monarchy: ". . . A suspicious *Verwilderung* of (inherited) symbols. . . . The word of the Lord was rare in those days. . . . The 'edifice of meaning' had been radically transformed." *Theologie des Alten Testaments* I,¹ (Munich: Chr. Kaiser Verlag 1957), p. 47.

29. "In primal mythos a cult-community celebrates the truth in which it is founded and 'assembled' (Heraclitus) as the actualization of a theophany" (p. 168).

30. The existentialist view does not sufficiently recognize the time category in which we are saved. It is doubtful whether on Heidegger's premises we can reach a satisfactory view as to how and why this (existentialist) interpretation can be understood "as an interpretation of history (*Geschichte*) in our dealing with time itself" (Fuchs, p. 175). It does not make clear that we can be joined to God not only morally and metaphysically, but also historically.

against existing patterns, wars upon inherited symbols and images. All this it can do because, as he says, it arises from a level where "the forms of life are fluid." The place of the myth is to Fuchs, "where the law of the *Grundlosen* rules."[31]

We would stress the fact that, in the realm of second causes, Jesus' visionary apocalyptic was conditioned by the cultural disorder and incoherence of his time. An older way of life had bcome increasingly nonviable. Older stabilities had been shaken. This carried with it both social and psychological disorders. The new sense of life and the world represented by Jesus inevitably brought about conflict in society and family. To those caught up in the Gospel, the old order of life would be seen as coming to an end. The new powers associated with the Gospel would inevitably require transcendental and miraculous expression. Jesus' message arose not first of all as an expression of freedom from the law, but as a message to those for whom the law had lost its meaningfulness. It was a message not first of all against the Pharisees, but for the poor and those who hungered for righteousness.

Though Jesus saw the crisis of his time and the ensuing redemption in mythological terms, we can recognize realistic elements in and through his sayings and action. He used the potent imagery of the national hope of his people, social symbol which had the power to ignite passion and precipitate division. As O. Betz and W. R. Farmer have argued, in the light of the religiopolitical holy-war activism of both Qumran and the Zealots, Jesus could use holy-war motifs in a way which was both mythological and immediately relevant.[32] It was inevitable that his goals should be confused with those of the Zealots by friend and foe alike. The Zealots were not secular brigands, but, like the early Maccabees, men like Phineas, zealous for the purity of the camp and consumed with zeal for the house of the Lord. As Betz says of Qumran, "The religious and political moments are indistinguishably bound up with each other."[33]

Jesus uses cosmic-demonological categories to interpret his historical activity, with respect to both his healings and his polemic.[34] He voices Yahweh's supreme controversy with his people and presents historical judgment and social futurities and outcomes in apocalyptic terms.[35] The say-

31. P. 169.

32. O. Betz, "Jesu Heiliger Krieg," *Novum Testamentum* 2 (1957):117-37; W. R. Farmer, *Maccabees, Zealots and Josephus* (New York: Cambridge University Press, 1956), chap. 8.

33. "Jesu," p. 117. E. Stauffer presents a strong case for Jesus' political concern, especially by exploiting the latter's *Hirtenpolemik* in the Fourth Gospel. *Jesus* (Bern, 1957), pp. 74-76. He rightly subordinates this area of Jesus' attention to larger issues, but we find it difficult to follow him in the way he does it—that is, by placing Jesus' self-identification in the center of the picture.

ings of Jesus which speak of the presence of the Kingdom determine for us the sense of those sayings which relate to its future. For as Ph. Vielhauer has noted, the two types of sayings—in contradiction to much two-age eschatology—are interfused with each other.[36] The realism of Jesus' outlook is further confirmed by the new evidence that his beatitude on the poor has in view the poor in its primary sense.[37]

There is a curious correlation between the apocalyptic transcendence of Jesus' gospel and his earthly realism—one could almost say his humanism or secular sensitivity. By comparison with the pieties of his time, his outlook is that of the layman. He had an empirical outlook, an emancipated sanity, and a corresponding "modernism" of rhetorical expression which almost suggest the category of a Jewish *Aufklärung*. All this, we say, is paradoxically related to a very high eschatology.

We find the antecedents for this in what Gerhard von Rad says about the creative and humanistic period in Israel after the founding of the monarchy, and in the "new spirit" reflected in the work of the Yahwist and the David narratives. The most important thing here, says Gerhard von Rad, is this:

> ... Jahweh's action embraces every department of life, the wholly secular as well as the sacral—there is, in fact, a certain eagerness to discover it out in the secular world. It is only here that the belief—already latent in principle in the earliest Jahwism—that Jahweh is the cause of all things, finds its proper form.[38]

Von Rad goes on to show that while Yahweh's control is located in the human heart, the person is not seen as a "religious character." It is rather that Jahweh "in order to direct history . . . uses them, their hearts and their resolutions."[39] This illuminates the outlook of Jesus. In his vision, also, all *Lebensbereiche* are brought under the control of God, and this determines the scope and original power of his eschatology.

---

34. See J. M. Robinson, *The Problem of History in Mark* (London: SCM, 1956), pp. 34, 42, 47 (also in Robinson's *The Problem of History in Mark and Other Marcan Studies* [Philadelphia: Fortress Press, 1982]); and his "Jesus' Understanding of History," *Journal of Biblical Religion* (1955):19.

35. This theme is developed in my *Otherworldliness and the New Testament* (London: SCM, 1954), chap. 3; German translation, *Weltfremdes Christentum?* (Göttingen: Vandenhoeck & Ruprecht, 1958).

36. "Gottesreich und Menschensohn in der Verkündigung Jesu," in W. Schneemelcher, ed., *Festschrift für G. Dehn* (1957), pp. 77–78.

37. E. Percy, *Die Botschaft Jesu* (1953), pp. 45–81; H. Braun, *Spätjüdischhäretischer und frühchristlicher Radikalismus* 2 (1957), p. 73, and n. 3.

38. *Old Testament Theology,* tr. D. M. G. Stalker (New York: Harper & Row, 1965), 1:53.

39. Ibid.

VI. ESCHATOLOGICAL IMAGERY AND
EARTHLY CIRCUMSTANCE

Our discussion has pointed to several criteria for distinguishing the most significant Jewish and Christian types of eschatology. Before turning to this, we may well remind ourselves of prevailing classifications. Most familiar, no doubt, is the schematization of our material based on doctrine as found in Charles, Volz, Oesterley, and similar interpreters. The chief interest here is in the transition from the older prophetic eschatology to the late type characterized by its transcendental portrayal of the New Age and its catastrophic inauguration, the place made for Satan, demons, and angels, and the incorporation of the doctrine of the resurrection. Distinctions are noted in texts representing this later type with respect to such issues as particularism versus universalism, resurrection versus immortality; the interim state, the role of the Messiah or Son of Man, if any, the relation of the Days of the Messiah to the Age to Come, and so forth."[40]

We are also familiar with analysis of eschatological features in terms of genetic study and antecedents. Another point of view which would repay further study is that of form and *Sitz-im-Leben* of the texts: prophetic oracle, testament, apocalypse proper, psalm, doxology, cult-recitation, paraenesis, works of literary pretension. When we have to do with this last category, it is of interest to note the various rhetorical traditions. One can identify such matters as self-conscious authorship, differing as it does in such cases as those of ben Sira, Philo, and Hermas; Hellenistic literary convention, as in the Sibylline Oracles or, outside of Christianity, Vergil's Fourth Eclogue; popular fabling color as in Fourth Ezra[41] or the New Testament apocrypha; veins of cosmological curiosity; various hieratic and hymnic genres (Ignatius),[42] and advent encomiums. All such differences of context are to be taken into account by the interpreter, for the various dualisms presupposed differ from one another with respect to world view

---

40. See the classifications set forth by Carl Steuernagel, "Die Strukturlinien der Entwicklung der jüdischen Eschatologie," in *Festschrift Alfred Bertholet* (1950), pp. 479–87. He first distinguishes between 1) national, 2) individual, and 3) universal or transcendental eschatologies, and then between 1) those identified with this world, and 2) those identified with conditions above this world with respect to either time or space. Each of these five patterns has its own course of development related to new historical circumstances, but these *Entwicklunslinien* also merge with each other in various ways.

41. Note the secular motifs in the *adunata*, 4:51–5: 13; 6: 21–24; and the metamorphosis of the woman representing Zion.

42. Cf. Carl Schneider, *Geistesgeschichte des antiken Christentums* II (1954), pp. 52–53.

(world-indifference, world-loathing, etc.), vitality, conventionality, and seriousness.

We wish, however, to emphasize another approach to the matter, one which, in effect, includes these others. The main thesis is that the most significant Jewish and Christian texts are those in which the redemptive assurance and hope are brought to bear upon the totality of the human situation, including not only the individual soul but society, not only the party or sect or nation but all mankind, not only history but creation, and all focused upon the present *kairos* in its most circumstantial and somatic reality. Many of our texts fail to meet such a test through one or another limitation of partiality or abstraction.

The matter may be explored by calling attention to the chief aspects of significant social symbol. These aspects are six in number. The first two are familiar. Social symbol is group-binding and time-binding. Our eschatological myth at its best is group-binding in a universal sense. It dramatizes the potential unity not only of sect, party, or nation. In binding time, it reaches back to include and make contemporary the whole past, returning not only to Sinai but to Adam and to the creation itself. The third aspect of significant social symbol is its immediate rootedness in and relevance to the contemporary life situation. Only so is the inherited imagery and myth quickened and potent for the society in question. At this point, much eschatology suffers, either because a legalist emphasis inhibits immediacy or because only a segment of contemporary need is addressed. Social symbol, in the fourth place, draws its greater power from the impact and presentness of transhistorical reality, that is, the immediacy of God in the symbol. This aspect is forfeited in our writings when the divine operation in the present is attenuated by legal, sapiential, or gnostic versions which qualify God's freedom or concern in the actual scene. The fifth aspect is the rhetorical: the symbol in question is constituted of dramatic media, heavily charged with associations reflecting the plenitude of the moral and affective life of the group and its past. It thus has an evocative and, as it were, explosive force as a means of communication and shock. Evidently a great deal of the eschatological imagery of our period fails here as derivative, secondhand, or esoteric. Finally, significant social symbol is not merely emotional, but cognitive. It embodies declaration and witness about the world and history of one kind or another. It represents wisdom, and not merely excitement. The genesis and role of myth is a matter of human *orientation*.

We may sum up by saying that our eschatological writings should be subjected to a double test. 1) Do they relate their assurances fully, or only partially, to man's historical life and need?[43] 2) Do they envision a fulfillment which involves the redemption not only of man, but of the creation?[44] By these tests, various of our texts fall short, and often the limitation of their scope corresponds to a weakness in imagery and rhetoric.

Thus, Wisdom and gnosticizing eschatologies, Jewish and Christian, restrict their goals too much to the individual and his inwardness, or to the esoteric group, and lack the cosmic teleology, and this is true in part of the Fourth Gospel. On the other hand, the systematically dualistic apocalypses, while they include the cosmic dimension, rise from sectarian, particularist, ascetic, or martyrological motives and reflect this in their partisan and otherworldly hereafter. The emphasis is more on the glory of the Most High in his retribution on the foe than on his glorious reign in a redeemed order. The eschatologies which glorify the law and the priesthood abstract from the full reality of the past, and thus deprive themselves of the nourishment of the taproot of Israel's total *Heilsgeschichte*.

Those expressions of Christian hope are most vital which relate themselves most fully to the biblical past. So Paul gives substance to his expectation of the renewal of the creation and of man by appealing back to David, to Moses, to Abraham, to Adam, and to the creation itself. Normative Christian eschatology related itself to a total human history in three respects: by this inclusive backward retrospect to Adam; by its implicit or explicit concern for the Gentiles; and by its responsible relation to the contemporary life situation, understood in its secular, as well as its religious aspects.

Thus the need to which it answered—the problem of man's self-understanding, or the religious crisis of the time—involved not only the individual but society, not only the religious, inward dimension but the public dimension, not only the present but the past, and not only man but nature. The impulse of the early Christian hope could not be satisfied with inwardness or a spiritual salvation. It required a new creation, but one represent-

43. The profound realism, both social and existential, of early Christian literature is a main point in Erich Auerbach's comparison of these writings with contemporary pagan work. See his comparison of pericopes in the Gospels and aspects of Paul's letters with the writings of Tacitus, Petronius, and Ammianus Marcellinus, *Mimesis* (Princeton: Princeton University Press, 1946), chaps. 2–3.

44. For an example of the holistic grasp of the redemption of history and nature, of this age and the age to come, we may point to Isa. 24–27: 1) earth and man, 24:5–6; 2) earth and cosmic-astral powers, 24:4c, 21; 3) Israel and the nations, 25:6–8; 4) this life and that of the resurrection, 25:6–8; 26:19; 5) the glorified earth, 25:6; 6) focus on the present actual situation, 27. (For the two Leviathans and the dragon, refer to the Diadochan states). See O. Procksch, *Theologie des Alten Testaments* (1950), p. 411; S. B. Frost, *Old Testament Apocalyptic* (London: Epworth, 1952), pp. 145–56.

ing the fulfillment of the old.[45] It is not surprising that such a total hope could only find adequate expression in a transcendental mythical statement. Yet such vision, though by its nature it dissolved ordinary relations of time, space, and causation, was nevertheless rooted in historical realities and could therefore later be translated and applied to ongoing circumstances.

45. What Edmond Jacob says of Jewish apocalyptic holds true here: "As Yahweh is the God who creates life, the catastrophic aspect of eschatology could never be the last word of his coming. The essential place is occupied by the notions of new creation and restoration. That is why the cleavage between history and eschatology is never radical." *Theology of the Old Testament,* tr. A. W. Heathcote and P. J. Allcock (London: Hodder & Stoughton, 1958), p. 318.

7

Apocalyptic Rhetorics

The metaphor of the Apocalypse is our best model for viewing our contemporary human condition. It alone gives us a large and flexible mythic form that is grand enough to allow a full expression of our agonies and aspirations . . . responsive to the major cataclysms of twentieth-century life and death.

Earl Rovit, "On the Contemporary Apocalyptic Imagination"

Some are there still (in prison), having spent the whole of Advent in prison. Of the others, there cannot be anyone who has not either in his work or in his private life had some sort of experience of the increasingly impatient attacks by the forces of the Antichrist.

Dietrich Bonhoeffer, 1937

I. LANGUAGE AT ITS LIMITS

There are veiled powers that live our lives; there are arcane transactions beneath the surface of experience that make fate for us; there are buried hierophanies and scenarios which are still potent in our orientation to existence. All this is the domain of apocalyptic encounter and utterance. Prophecy, art, and poetry are fed by these dynamics, but in times of crisis when continuities are broken, we are immediately exposed to them and they find their own archetypal voice.

One such archaic motif is that of spiritual Armageddon, or war in heaven, involving the living. To give a concrete example, I cite my own transcription of a World War I experience in which the actual duress took on mythical extrapolation.

> There we marched out on haunted battle-ground,
> There smelled the strife of gods, were brushed against
> By higher beings, and were wrapped around
> With passions not of earth, all dimly sensed.

153

> There saw we demons fighting in the sky
> And battles in aerial mirage,
> The feverish Véry lights proclaimed them by,
> Their tramplings woke our panting, fierce barrage.
>
> Their tide of battle, hither, thither, driven
> Filled earth and sky with cataclysmic throes,
> Our strife was but the mimicry of heaven's
> And we the shadows of celestial foes.[1]

In these lines it is to be noted, however, we have apocalyptic only at a second remove, in a literary mode. The initial utterance of the apocalyptist lacks the cultured medium of verse and the persona of the poet. It is archetypal and prepersonal. In the Old Testament, this differentiates it from prophecy, in which the identity of the seer is prominent and in which parallelistic style is usual.

This observation points us immediately to the chief difficulty of our topic: the variety of our texts, but especially the variety of levels, psychological and linguistic, through which primary apocalyptic vision has been mediated. Archaic motifs become literary, primal myth is subject to displacement, momentous hierophanies are historized and receive innunmerable ad hoc revisions and interpretations. We are confronted with kalaidoscopic rearrangements of a numinous repertoire in both ancient and modern apocalyptic. In these mutations we recognize also, of course, vast differences in quality, whether assessed in terms of reality-sense or literary force. Going behind all such secondary or derivative rhetorics, the present paper will seek to characterize apocalyptic utterance in its initial phase.

Two main types of criteria have been used in identifying apocalyptic texts of the ancient period, and both have proved unsatisfactory. A list of "features" can be compiled (dualism, pseudonymity), but these are found to be mainly thematic, and in any case external and involved many exceptions. Or, a literary test of *Gattung* can be sought, and then we find that there are many *Gattungen* and that these are also present in nonapocalyptic material. We must therefore try to find more decisive criteria, and this means going behind our transmitted writings, or further upstream. Therefore I am not dealing directly here with such evolved texts as the First Book of Enoch, or the Book of Revelation, or Blake's "Four Zoas." We should first seek to locate the genesis of this unique language mode.

The impasse in our assessment of biblical apocalyptic has been recog-

---

1. "Interlude," in *Battle-Retrospect and Other Poems* (New Haven: Yale University Press, 1923), p. 31. Cf. "Armageddon," in my book *Arachne: Poems* (New Haven: Yale University Press, 1928), pp. 45–49.

nized by leading scholars[2] and comes to expression in Klaus Koch's title, *Ratlos vor der Apokalyptik*.[3] This situation points to the wisdom of placing our topic in a wider context. We should study analogous texts of any period, including our own, and look for tools, approaches, and methods that may be carried over from contemporary literary criticism toward the illumination of the older writings. Even within the ancient period, Hans Dieter Betz has urged that early apocalyptic writings be viewed in the context of the whole development of Hellenistic-Oriental syncretism.[4] But modern investigation of similar writings has refined its own sophistications, such as those bearing on the psychology of authorship, the social psychology of millenarian and utopian vision and fantasy, the phenomenology of genres in relation to views of time, and all such matters as symbol, myth, and archetype.

But, contrariwise, the student of modern apocalyptic has reason to bring the ancient exemplars into his purview. The chaotic diversity of the modern material impels him to look for some kind of foil to aid him in his assessment. One consideration is that these ancient texts are often the quarry in which the modern apocalyptic imagination finds its vehicles. Thus Northrop Frye speaks of the Book of Revelation from one point of view as "our grammar of apocalyptic imagery."[5] But apart from this, in our preoccupation with nineteenth- and twentieth-century types of apocalyptic, we should be on guard against any too limited context. Our own particular *Zeitgeist* may lead to a fascination with contmporary mood and idiom and thus blind us to wider bearings. The student of the more recent texts identified with epiphany, catastrophe, anomie, and surrealism can understand the material better, precisely at the literary level, by bringing it into relation with analogous works of a differrent epoch.

The task of correlation before us, evidently, should be on the agenda not only of theologians, but also of secular "comparative literature." But since the most important ancient writings in question are biblical, this latter aspect of the task has been blocked, as in so many other areas involving

2. G. von Rad, *Theologie des Alten Testaments*, II, (Munich: Chr. Kaiser Verlag, 1965[4]), pp. 315, 330; P. Vielhauer, "Apocalypses and Related Subjects," in Edgar Hennecke and Wilhelm Schneemelcher, eds., *New Testament Apocrypha II* (Philadelphia: Westminster Press, 1965), p. 594; J. M. Schmidt, *Die jüdische Apokalyptik* (Neukirchen-Vluyn: Neukirchener Verlag, 1969), p. 313.

3. Gütersloh: Gerd Mohn, 1970. English translation by Margaret Kohl, *The Rediscovery of Apocalyptic* (London: SCM, 1972).

4. "Zum Problem des religionsgeschichtlichen Verständnisses der Apokalyptik," *Zeitschrift für Theologie und Kirche* 63(1966), pp. 391–409, esp. pp. 394, 409. English translation in *Journal for Theology and Church* 6(1969), pp. 134–56.

5. *Anatomy of Criticism* (Princeton: Princeton University Press, 1957), p. 141.

the Scriptures and their rhetorics. Significant confrontation of ancient and modern apocalyptic should identify some common level that goes beyond such surface similarities as derivative imagery or portrayal of cosmic disorder. We must also go beyond our usual Western literary categories. Academic canons have to be strained to deal with even modern apocalyptic writings, let alone the biblical. We must look to ultimate considerations about language itself and to the modes in which different apprehensions of reality come to speech. Particular rhetorics and genres are conditioned by varying presuppositions as to existence, and language is ontologically determined in ways that are prior to more observable features.

Since we are dealing with acts of the imagination and of language which break with the cultural patterns of their particular period, we should think of rhetorics here in terms that are more generic and fate-laden than those associated with humanistic categories. Therefore such terms as *existential, ontological,* and *archetypal* impose themselves, and these can be good tools for approaching apocalyptic, if we mean that everything is exposed and at stake. The total character of the apocalyptic crisis is well suggested in the theophany recorded in 2 Samuel:

> Then the earth reeled and rocked; . . .
> Then the channels of the sea were seen,
> the foundations of the world were laid bare (22:8, 16).

But with some alleged apocalyptic vision and writing it is still very much a question whether, in fact, *everything* is at stake, because it is very human to vociferate apocalyptically when something that we prize is taken away from us, whether a baby rattle or a bank account, whether our sense of class or national pride, or our sense of how things should be generally. The true apocalyptic seizure is something different from apoplexy! The rhetoric in either case may be dynamic, ultrarational, and even purple. But one should be able to tell the difference between the tantrums of a romantic who cannot bring the world to heel and the impersonal voice which speaks out of the crucible where the world is made and unmade.

In both ancient and modern apocalyptic, we recognize bastard exemplars, not deeply rooted in man's ultimate *aporia* but animated by some partisan grievance, or lacking in vitality in keeping with a schizoid departure from reality. In such cases the rhetoric moves toward the monological and toward manic fantasy. Yet the recurrence of "ranters," alarmists, and purveyors of "florid extremism" should not blind us to the healthy function of genuine transcendental apocalyptic.

II. ARCHAIC MOTIFS

Common to all true apocalyptic is a situation characterized by anomie, a loss of "world," or erosion of structures, psychic and cultural, with the consequent nakedness to Being or immediacy to the dynamics of existence.[6] Hence the rhetorics of this "panic" exposure in which all is at stake, involving antinomies of life and death, light and darkness, knowledge and nescience, order and chaos. And it can never be only a question of the individual. It is a juncture which renews the archaic crisis of all existence: that of survival, the viability of life.

Since inherited structures are forfeit, the only available dramatizations of the crisis or of any projectable "future" will necessarily have a *precultural* character (in the sense of a regression behind existing social conventions and symbolic patterns). Precultural, first, in a temporal sense: a return to archaic motifs and to deeply buried hierophanies of the group. But precultural also in the sense of a language responsive to the unmediated dynamics that underlie all Being and Becoming. But this means that the language is to that extent devoid of personal and current sociocultural features. It is a quasi-autonomous utterance, in this sense like the alien communication of pre-Columbian sculpture in which we sense the enigma of the unthought and the unthinkable. Thus a kind of archetypal idiom is required in such a crisis of meaning.

But this idiom and imagery cannot be wholly discontinuous with older categories of language and imagination. In Jewish apocalyptic, we can recognize a falling back, indeed, upon pre-Israelite motifs and a generic mythology of chaos and order. But this is filtered through Israel's own archetypal mythology. Frank M. Cross, Jr., points to the "old epic" of the nation and the wars of Yahweh, as well as to the royal ideology.[7] Though these motifs had, indeed, lived on in the prophets and psalmists, yet in apocalyptic they were taken up and transformed in a radically new setting. Contemporary apocalyptic, for its part, arises from epiphanic disclosures answering to our own dilemma. Here, too, anticultural iconoclasm opens

6. "Human life is reduced to real suffering, to hell, only when two ages, two cultures and religions overlap. . . . Now there are times when a whole generation is caught in this way between two ages, two modes of life, with the consequence that it loses all power to understand itself and has no standard, no security, no single acquiescence." Hermann Hesse, *Steppenwolf* (1927), cited by Walter Wink, "Apocalypse in Our Time," *Katallagete* 3 (1970):13.

7. "New Directions in the Study of Apocalyptic," *Apocalypticism* 6 (1969): 161–65.

the way for repossession of archaic motifs, but in a way conditioned by the modern sensibility and modern apperception.

The centrality of the category of "revelation," in the sense of ecstatic disclosure, is evident in the term *apocalyptic,* as in other indications in our writings. The ancient texts testify clearly to this kind of origin, whether of their initial core or of later strata. Even where the category of vision becomes a convention, scholars agree that the writers not only took over earlier theophanies, but that they were themselves visionaries. Our first extended texts, moreover, arose in a period when the religiosity of antiquity turned towards esoteric disclosures of higher wisdom, especially from the Orient, and when, thanks to the diffusion of protoscientific lore about man, nature, and the cosmos, the whole theater of existence required new and more sophisticated versions of salvation.

The apocalyptic seers therefore recapture the archaic cosmic-mythological motifs of Israel, but now in terms of the Hellenistic outlook according to which man's consciousness and fate were associated with the world elements and with astral and chthonic powers.[8] We can recognize a correspondence here with modern apocalyptic in its breaking down of the barriers between man and "nature," exemplified in current space fiction and ecological consciousness, as well as in the thought of Teilhard de Chardin. All apocalyptic moves toward this cosmic scope and repertoire. Not only are nonhuman realities evoked, but human issues are inseparably linked with these. Modern apocalyptic will have the same scope, going beyond the anthropological, but its cosmic extrapolation will of course differ in view of our different, modern cosmology and reality-sense. One can thus distinguish the apocalyptic theater and dramatis personae of different epochs, even with respect to moderns like Blake, Nietzsche, and Yeats.

It is necessary at this point to confront the vexed question as to the relation of apocalyptic to history, and indeed to reality in general. Here we meet the recurrent disparagement of apocalyptic associated with such terms as *dualistic, pessimistic, esoteric, deterministic, ahistorical, escapist, fantastic, compensatory.* The issue arises with respect to both ancient and modern versions. It bears directly on our interest here in the rhetorical

---

8. For abundant documentation of these aspects of Jewish apocalyptic and its employment of popular motifs and styles of the period, see Martin Hengel, *Judentum und Hellenismus* (Tübingen: J. C. B. Mohr [Paul Siebeck], 1969), pp. 319–94. English translation by John Bowden, *Judaism and Hellenism I* (Philadelphia: Fortress Press 1974), pp. 153–217.

aspect, for it is a question of "language and reality" and of respect or dis-respect for imaginative discourse per se, or for any transcendental symbol. We must, of course, discriminate among our texts by the kind of tests we employ with any fabulation. But we should not come to them with fixed or anachronistic axioms as to what is real, what is history, what is humanly effective.

To illustrate from our older writings: there is no doubt that after the Jewish exile sectarian groups arose which dissociated themselves from the priestly theocracy. They kept alive the eschatological hopes of the prophets and added proto-apocalyptic sections to their writings. This development became highly significant in the Maccabean period, and their whole attitude can be seen as an "escape into myth" consequent upon a pessimistic view of the situation.

Recent study of the transition from prophecy to apocalyptic in Israel has done much to clarify this picture. We may take von Rad's position as representative of the kind of disparagement mentioned above. He sees apocalyptic here as "basically tending to an ahistorical thinking," and its correlation of universal history with zoology and demonology as "leading to a quasi-hybrid form of universal gnosis."[9] Such scholars as Koch, Hengel, and Schmidt have countered all such depreciation. Koch denies that the seers adopt only "a spectator's view of history."[10] Hengel points out that it is in fact other movements in the Hellenistic period which for-feited a true sense of historical action, with their views of life as subject to the caprice of Tyche or to astral determination.[11] Schmidt shows how all such disparagements of Jewish apocalyptic are connected with one or an-other *parti pris,* such as those which disesteem postexilic developments in Judaism, or insist on the direct relation of Christianity to the Hebrew prophets.[12] Hengel, moreover, has shown the many interconnections of apocalyptic with the non-Jewish cultures of the period, thus making it clear that this kind of imaginative wisdom and rhetoric spoke to a real and fateful mentality widely influential.[13]

9. *Theologie des Alten Testaments,* 2:321, 318.
10. *Ratlos vor der Apokalyptik,* pp. 40–45.
11. *Judentum und Hellenismus,* p. 381.
12. *Die jüdische Apokalyptik,* pp. 306–12.
13. See n. 8, above. We should include with these other correctives the contribu-tion of Paul D. Hanson. He has undercut the familiar but superficial view that the dualistic-mythological features of apocalyptic were only late and peripheral elements taken over from third- and second-century B.C. Zoroastrianism. Besides studying, like Otto Ploeger, the real situation out of which apocalyptic developed after the Exile, he has documented by contextual and by prosodic evidence the reappropriation by

The upshot is that we should not disparage apocalyptic over against either prophecy or eschatology. It spoke to its own historical situation and the existing sense of reality. It pioneered the first universal view of history including all peoples and all times. It took history with utter seriousness, confronting the seemingly total disaster of the present and assigning meaning and hope to it in terms of the wider cosmic drama. Those symbols, motifs, and styles which strike us as fantastic spoke effectively to the consciousness and apperception of many. The fact is that our ability to understand ancient apocalyptic requires an analogous visionary capacity operating in our own setting. The great example here is Albert Schweitzer. One can illustrate by his epiphanic aphorism: "The late-Jewish Messianic world-view is the crater from which burst forth the flame of the eternal religion of love."[14]

III. PRECULTURAL UTTERANCE

If we then identify the matrix of apocalyptic language with situations of anomie, what special kinds of rhetoric will we expect to find? What is the linguistic gesture of the zero-point, granting that such an expression is hyperbolic? I would like to press that in such occasions meaning can come through only in enigmatic ciphers drawn from outside the immediate cultural heritage. In the case of Israel, with the loss of continuities incident to the exile, Frank Cross finds the Book of Job paradigmatic. All categories in which meaning can be identified are wiped out, and the only voice Job can hear is that of the archaic thunder God, El or Ba'l, who speaks in enigmas of an ultimate premoral mystery.[15]

Especially as regards hope and future—as regards answers and solutions or deliverance—since everything is in jeopardy and since every trusted security is disallowed, therefore the only future that is possible can be in terms of the prodigy and the *miraculum*. The hierophany in this situation calls forth, as it were, nonlanguage, or rhetorics featured by enormity and paradox. In this situation of disorientation, vertigo, and weightlessness, there are not only no answers; there are no categories, no questions.

The account in the Second Chapter of Daniel is a perfect transcription

---

the visionary groups of the archaic cosmic and mythological motifs which had always been a part of Israel's heritage, and which now served a new need when the empirical prospects of the nation were in such disarray. See his *The Dawn of Apocalyptic* (Philadelphia: Fortress Press, 1979); also, "Jewish Apocalyptic Against Its Near Eastern Environment," *Revue Biblique*: 79 (1971).

14. *Out of My Life and Thoughts: An Autobiography* (New York: Holt, Rinehart & Winston, 1933), p. 69.

15. "New Directions," pp. 162–63.

of this situation. King Nebuchadnezzar wants an interpretation of his dream by the magicians, the enchanters, the sorcerers, and the Chaldeans, but he also threatens them with death unless they first tell him the dream. They answer him: "The thing that the king asks is difficult, and none can show it to the king except the gods, whose dwelling is not with flesh" (2:11). But "then the mystery was revealed to Daniel in a vision of the night" (2:19). It is, moreover, in keeping with the category of prodigy in which apocalyptic moves that his theophany climaxes in the vision of "a stone . . . cut out by no human hand," which smote the image representing the world empires of the East, a stone which then "became a great mountain and filled the whole earth" (2:34–35). Behind the historized narrative as we have it here, no doubt, we can recognize the original hierophany in this elemental nonhuman vision. Similarly, behind the psalm of blessing here put in the mouth of Daniel (vv. 20–23), we can perhaps catch echoes of the original mimetic acclamation, especially in the words "he changes times and seasons" and "he knows what is in the darkness."

Since sheer immediacy takes precedence over all else, the voice of the apocalyptist, in the initial phase, is like that associated with ecstatic hierophanies as they are documented in tribal ceremonies in early Israel and in the older strata of Greek religion. When the group is confronted by (enveloped in) the prodigious, the language response is that of acclamation, as the ritual response is enactment. The voice is the reflex of the event; it is the voice of the event. When the lightning and thunder occur the tribe identifies itself with the preternatural event by drums, gongs, and trumpet blasts. They enact the hierophany by magical mimesis.[16] The language of the shaman is transparent to the cosmic happening at the point where the world is made and unmade.

A few examples: The African tribesmen, at the height of the rite, make their acclamation "The Fathers are here!" Or, as Jacob exclaimed when the angels of God met him at Mahanaim, "This is God's host." Ernst Käsemann, in his sifting of the formal apocalyptic utterance of the earliest Christian prophets, notes the ecstatic *Maranatha*, a cry that went up in the Eucharistic gathering, in this situation with the meaning "The Lord is come," or "The Lord is here."[17] The Lord is not only summoned ("Come, Lord") but acclaimed as present. Tradition-historical study of the Balaam

---

16. Cf. W. F. Otto, *Dionysos: Mythos und Kultus* (Frankfurt-am-Main: Klostermann, 1933), p. 45.

17. "Sentences of Holy Law in the New Testament" in *New Testament Questions of Today,* tr. W. J. Montague (Philadelphia: Fortress Press, 1969), pp. 69–70. Cf. G. Delling, *Worship in the New Testament* (Philadelphia: Westminster Press, 1962), pp. 69–70.

oracles in Numbers 23—24 no doubt points to their displacement and elaboration. But the phenomenology of ecstatic acclamation and magic blessing is reflected in the legend of Balaam, "who saw the vision of the Almighty, falling into a trance, but having his eyes open," especially in the cry "What hath God wrought!"

The language of the apocalyptist, in its initial phase, has this same mimetic character; it is the immediate register of the hierophany, where meaning speaks out of meaninglessness. As such, it is first of all acclamation that echoes and continues the event, the *miraculum*. It is reflexive, not reflective. The syntax is not discursive or poetic or dialogic in the first instance. It takes the form of exclamation, apostrophe, adjuration, vow, spell, curse, blessing. The language is part of the happening. As Wallace Stevens says in another key, "The poem is the cry of its occasion."[18]

For an example, we may turn to first of the dream-visions in the Book of Enoch.

> I had lain me down in the house of my grandfather Mahalalel, (when) I saw in a vision how the heaven collapsed and was borne off and fell to the earth. And when it fell to the earth I saw how the earth was swallowed up in a great abyss. . . . And thereupon a word fell into my mouth, and I lifted up (my voice) to cry aloud, and said: "The earth is destroyed" (83:3–5).

It is true that the apocalyptist *writes* in a postprimitive situation, and is no shaman. But he writes in a cultural vacuum in which, as in the case of the "primitive," contextual meaning is weak, and his language has therefore a similarly autonomous character. Though he writes, I am convinced that this cultural medium of writing nevertheless incorporates mimetic and ecstatic utterance and formulas, whether originating in his own vision or in ancient hierophanies quickened in his own imaginative act.[19] The prophet, on the other hand, though he speaks out of a broken order, retains his self-consciousness and identity and appeals to a sociohistorical covenant. His theophany comes to him in the language mode of dialogue.

---

18. "An Ordinary Evening in New Haven," in *The Auroras of Autumn* (New York: Knopf, 1950), p. 132.

19. Aage Bentzen, who notes that "apocalyptists are not ecstatic prophets but learned men of letters" nevertheless agrees with Bousset that "their visions are not only forms" and that "real experiences lie behind the visions of 4 Ezra. . . . The apocalyptists have also had dreams and visions, seen angelic figures, and heard angelic voices." *Introduction to the Old Testament I* (Copenhagen: G. E. C. Gad, 1952), pp. 257–58. Cf. L. Hartman, "An author who uses well-established, conventional literary forms for rendering visions may nevertheless cast his own visionary experiences in precisely these forms which he has taken over." *Prophecy Interpreted* (Lund: C. W. K. Gleerup, 1966), p. 105. Also Schmidt, *Die jüdische Apokalyptik*, pp. 279–81.

In the case of the apocalyptist, no such traditional vehicles or filters of the hierophany are available. He is thrown back on older archetypes and their arcane utterance.[20] If he appeals to a covenant, the analogy is with Job's league "with the stones of the field" (5:23), or with the "eternal covenant" with the creation celebrated in the hymn in the Manual of Discipline of the Qumran community and in its collection of psalms, the Hodayot.[21] It is in keeping with this that the persona of the seer is ignored or identified with some ancient prototype of Wisdom.

It is also in keeping with this that at its very birth this kind of utterance already exhibits astonishment at the mystery of language and concern for the esoterics of revelation and interpretation. This latter takes on elaborate development with the "machinery" of visions, auditions, mediaries, mysteries, parables, heavenly books, scrolls. But this fascination with the processes and media of *knowing,* with words and numerals and signs, is an index of the precultural locus of this literary type. We find something like it in Samuel Beckett's fictions in which the anonymous protagonist wrestles with the elements of language. I return to the essential point that the rhetorics of apocalyptic are peculiar in that they dramatize the group hierophany in a situation of broken continuities. To use one formulation, the language-event in question brings ontological happening to speech. It is true that our existing apocalyptic works include superimposed layers of later interpretation and adaptation to various genres. We see here the progressive culturizing of the initial vision. But even these later strata are shaped by it. Decisive for that original moment was the fact that *all* was forfeit to chaos. Therefore the total or cosmic reference of the language and its cosmological-mythical character.

All the categories are in question: *space* (as then apprehended), with its celestial, mundane, and chthonic realms and agencies. *Time* also is in question, because the very existence and survival of the group is in jeopardy; and past, present, and future have become enigmatic. *Causation* is in question, because the powers of the Dragon and of nonbeing are over-

---

20. "Apocalyptic, unlike prophecy, does not stress Israel's *Heilsgeschichte.* In Daniel, for instance, there is no typology of the old Exodus and the new, no reinterpretation (*Vergegenwärtigung*) of the sacred history of God's dealing with his people, Israel. Apocalyptic writers viewed history in *universal* terms—as a historical and even a cosmic drama which moves from the absolute beginning of time (creation) to the absolute end. . . . In apocalyptic the chaos myth is not historized to refer to saving events of Israel's history (as in Second Isaiah); rather, chaos imagery is used to portray the cosmic rebellion, the demonic struggle which characterizes the whole historical drama from beginning to end." B. W. Anderson, *Creation and Chaos* (New York: Association Press, 1967), pp. 136–37.

21. Cf. my *Early Christian Rhetoric: The Language of the Gospel* (Cambridge: Harvard University Press, 1971), pp. 111–15. Also, D. Rössler, *Gesetz und Geschichte* (Neukirchen-Vluyn: Neukirchener Verlag, 1960), p. 54.

whelmingly felt. Witness here the ambiguity of encounter with the gods or the prodigious, as instanced in the cases of Dionysus, Vishnu, and Shiva, and Job's antagonist. In passing we may note how wrestling with these categories led to various forms of refinement: in the case of space, cosmic geographies; in the case of time, periodizations; in the case of causation, portrayals of mythological agencies. But all such curiosities and calculations were, in the main, existentially motivated.

I find support for my theme in Ernst Käsemann's view of the earliest Christian apocalyptic. The ecstatic formulas of the Christian prophets have their context in eschatological throes. We do not have personalized witness, rather beatitudes, woes, exclamations, *Sätze heiligen Rechtes*—that is, autonomous divine law. Soteriology is general and total, cosmic before it is anthoropological. Ecclesiology is supramundane and mythical (not excluding the actual and historical, but subsuming them).[22]

The archaic and acultural character of the rhetorics is especially clear in the large role played by the nonhuman world, the imagery drawn from the inanimate order—stone, mountain, tree, fire, celestial bodies—meteorology, as well as from mythical terriology—dragon, beasts, insects. Associations with the sea, the clouds, earthquake, eclipse, storm, and whirlwind are typical. It is in the nature of the case that cosmic transaction takes precedence over the political-historical, or that the latter is extrapolated into the former. Under various images the transaction moves through death to life, through chaos to order, and the recurrent pattern is that of war and victory, though more human models may shape the vision, such as those of childbirth or of harvest.

If we have the appearance of a human figure, it is in conjunction with the clouds of heaven, and this goes back to some primordial hierophany of enthronement conveying the *miraculum* of cosmic reversal and deliverance. Presumably the instant acclamation that accompanied it has been disguised in the process of adaptation, but had some such form as is found repeatedly in Daniel and in the whole succession of apocalyptic writings: "(Thy) dominion is an everlasting dominion! (7:14)."

IV. GENRES AND STYLES

This paper has confined itself largely to the underlying impulse and mode of apocalyptic discourse. In this respect what has been said applies to both ancient and modern periods. It would be another task to show how such utterance becomes culturized and diversified. The developed texts exhibit successive layers of adaptation, evidencing the ways in which the enigmatic

22. *Op. cit.,* pp. 66–81.

hierophany could take on public resonance and communicability. Here would be the place to discriminate the various genres and styles that have seemed especially predestined to serve this task. I would identify three language modes particularly: the vision, the dialogue, and the narrative.

That such writings come to us in the literary mode of a vision or sequence of visions, rather than ecstatic acclamation, is understandable enough. The group keeps alive the hierophany and its voice by the authority of a witness. The dramatized vision carries over the original transhistorical and transsubjective encounter. Angelic instruction or dream interpretation now include aspects of wisdom, mandate, paraenesis, and consolation—still in dynamic and mythological tenor—which carry the potency of the original event.

The dialogue mode, again, so recurrent a feature in our literature, dialogue between the revealer and the human medium or between cosmic powers, is again a mutation from the original encounter. In that situation there is no dialogue, only immediacy. When dialogue appears in apocalyptic writings, it differs from that in prophecy or liturgy. Dialogue in the Book of Revelation, for example, is different from that in the Gospel of John. The latter dialogue, with all its antinomies and ironies, is not charged with the same kind of numinous tension associated with the cosmic theater and the preternatural voices and cries of the Apocalypse.

The narrative mode, again—recall its place in Daniel or in heavenly travelogues or in rehearsals of world epochs—is another category in which the original vision is extrapolated and turned into literature. In keeping with its source, this kind of narrative, whether retrospective or predictive, has a cosmic scene and tells of agencies and events which partake of the fateful and prodigious.

V. THE MODERN CATASTROPHIC IMAGINATION

The term *apocalyptic* is widely used today in connection with modern situations and events, attitudes and anticipations, arts and letters. Studies of the modern apocalyptic imagination cite works of a long lineage preoccupied with absolute evil and the end of the world, works associated not only with religious sects, but with sociol-ecological and political alarms, if not hysteria.[23] The relation of all such modern apocalyptic to ancient apoc-

23. See R. W. B. Lewis, "Days of Wrath and Laughter," in *Trials of the Word* (New Haven: Yale University Press, 1965), pp. 184–35; E. Rovit, "On the Contemporary Apocalyptic Imagination," *The American School* 37(1968): 453–68; G. Boklund, "Time Must Have a Stop: Apocalyptic Thought and Expression in the Twentieth Century," *Denver Quarterly* 2(1967), pp. 69–98; W. Wink, "Apocalypse," pp. 13–18; Frye, *Anatomy of Criticism*, pp. 141–46; T. J. Altizer, "Imagination and Apocalypse," *Sound* 53(1970): 398–12.

alyptic is ambiguous. Biblical symbols may be invoked, but often only in an eclectic way. The visionary mode is certainly common to both. The modern texts widely focus only on the negative or catastrophic aspect.

Attention to the modern apocalyptic novel should be illuminating. This is well represented by Nathaniel West's *The Day of the Locust*,[24] John Barth's *The Sot-Weed Factor*,[25] and Thomas Pynchon's *V*.[26] The use of the category of apocalyptic to describe these novels surely has some justi- fication here, as with other novels often so characterized, by Ralph Ellison, Joseph Heller, and other authors. The revelatory test is met by the presence of aspects of the surreal, oneiric, and hallucinatory. Thus Pynchon's V (the book's "heroine") represents an epiphany of the monstrous, the "nameless horror," and its masquerades. The mythological test is met by the evident regression to archaic cyphers of order and chaos. So also with West's use of properties from the Apocalypse of John, as in his very title. The feature of catastrophe, also in its imminent aspect, is prominent in such fictions: witness the projected "burning of Los Angeles" in West's novel, or the anticipated "loosening of Satan" incident to the universalized race riot in Harlem at the close of Ellison's *Invisible Man*.

One misses two things in this kind of writing, however, and one could include such films as Bergman's *The Hour of the Wolf* or a play like van Itallie's *American Hurrah*. Should we not keep the term *apocalyptic* for that which is total, cosmic, and ultimate? In West's novel, the central char- acter, who is an artist, would paint the fury of the demonic throng, "ap- preciating its awful, anarchic power, and aware that they had it in them to destroy civilization." These novels move political satire into a mythical and apocalyptic lighting. But even with this surrealist overtone, the fate of civilization is not the same thing as the fate of all life and creation. The overthrow of sociocultural tyrannies, even in Blake and Nietzsche, does not engage the ultimate crisis. But these modern works explore the task of identifying and naming that crisis, even by such extreme strategies as those represented by Genet in his reversals of good and evil, honor and shame, order and subversion.

It is true that the novels in question suggest something of what I have called the precultural and elemental vision of apocalyptic. Natural forms take the place of men in *The Day of the Locust*. Both Barth and Pynchon employ the motif of the monstrous in seeing men as synthetic, reified, as falling apart into plastic or glass or mineral nullity. Gunnar Boklund offers

24. New York: New Directions, 1950.
25. New York: Doubleday, 1960.
26. Philadelphia: J. B. Lippincott, 1963.

illustrations from German expressionism. Thus Stefan George, in the poem, "Der Krieg" (1917), writes:

> Des Schöpfers hand entwischt rast eigenmächtig
> Unform von blei und blech, gestäng und rohr.[27]

Man's cosmic inherence in more than this negative sense comes to expression in space-science fiction, as it did with Blake in the celestial and meteorological mode of the "Four Zoas."

But the second thing we miss in most modern apocalyptic is the phase of miraculous renovation and that world affirmation which has gone through the experience of world negation. A hierophany properly means both Naysaying and Yea-saying, and the catastrophic imagination alone is therefore not genuinely apocalyptic. At best the novels we have noted keep alive the positive pole by stylistic strategies associated with grim humor, facetiousness, and the grotesque.[28] But the full apocalyptic scenario should include salvation as well as judgment, the new age as well as the old.

We find this in one vein of modern apocalyptic, that which balances world dissolution with palingenesis as with Blake, or which overcomes contemporary nihilism by epiphany in the line of Nietzsche. Anticipating the riper cultural anomie of today, Nietzsche combined a radical negation (based on his epiphany of the death of God) with a radical ecstatic affirmation voicing itself in the symbols of Eternal Return and the Overman. Thomas Altizer has asked whether we could not understand this movement, arising like ancient apocalyptic out of the breakdown of an earlier form of faith, as one "which enlarges and yet reverses ancient apocalyptic forms and identities, and yet which nevertheless carries ancient apocalypticism to its own intrinsic conclusion."[29] Again I would say that such cultural iconoclasm is to be valued as an exploration of the real crisis and its solution. But the great reversal Nietzsche hails is not rooted in the ultimate anomie in which all is at stake. Secular versions of transcendence in the line which runs from Blake to Nietzsche to Yeats were too largely determined by the affective and aesthetic apperception of the period. Moreover, the pattern of Hegelian dialectic and antithesis which Altizer employs does not do justice to the real continuity between old age and new age in ancient

27. "Escaped from the hand of the maker, nonform of lead and tin, of rod and tube, rage of their own volition." Quoted in Boklund, "Time Must Have a Stop," p. 88.

28. Well argued in the essay by Lewis cited in n. 23 above.

29. Paper read at the annual meeting of the Society of Biblical Literature, New York, October 1970. Altizer also commented that "old apocalypticism passes into new apocalypticism by way of a yet deeper interiorization and negation of itself."

apocalyptic, and abrogates the normative significance of those ancient hierophanies and texts with respect especially to our ultimate orientation in existence.

Certainly the modern cultural crisis occasions genuine archetypal vision and language. Where it is born out of an ultimate paroxysm and wrestling with meaninglessness and the viability of the human, it is fateful for any tomorrow. Viewed against the whole phenomenology of the biblical texts, however, the following questions arise:

1. *Psychologism versus a presubjective and total encounter.* The modern world has been fated with a burden of subjectivity—Enlightenment, individualism, Romanticism, existentialism—which canalizes our encounters with reality into forms of private and aesthetic epiphany. Thus the communal and human basis of true apocalyptic is handicapped.

2. *Aestheticism versus responsibility.* The hierophany of radical apocalyptic takes hold of man's will and intentionality, and not only of his vision. It is a question of our view of man. Husserl, Heidegger, and the new hermeneutics see man's being in terms of freedom and choice, of historicity in this sense. Much modern apocalyptic represents only the dramas of the imagination. Here we can oppose the apocalyptic reality of Joel:

> Multitudes, multitudes,
> in the valley of decision! . . .
> The sun and moon are darkened,
> and the stars withdraw their shining (3:14–15).

By this test,[30] most examples of the modern apocalyptic imagination fail to measure either the depth of the disorder or the operative agencies of the new creation.

---

30. *Decision* here, indeed, refers first of all to the divine judgment on the nations, but the mythological setting of cosmic convulsion evokes the *obligations* of a primordial covenant, older than those of Israel.